D1064944

The Maya

LOST WORLDS AND
MYSTERIOUS CIVILIZATIONS

Atlantis

Easter Island

El Dorado

The Maya

Nubia

Pompeii

Roanoke

Troy

LOST WORLDS AND MYSTERIOUS CIVILIZATIONS

The Maya

Shane Mountjoy

CHELSEA HOUSE
An Infobase Learning Company

The Maya
Copyright ©2012 by Infobase Learning

Chelsea House
An imprint of Infobase Learning
132 West 31st Street
New York NY 10001

Library of Congress Cataloging-in-Publication Data
Mountjoy, Shane, 1967–
  The Maya / by Shane Mountjoy.
    p. cm. — (Lost worlds and mysterious civilizations)
  Includes bibliographical references and index.
  ISBN 978-1-60413-976-1 (hardcover)
  1. Mayas—History. 2. Mayas—Antiquities. 3. Mayas—Social life and customs. I. Title.
  F1435.M78 2011
  972'.6—dc22   2011011616

Chelsea House books are available at special discounts when purchased in bulk quantities for businesses, associations, institutions, or sales promotions. Please call our Special Sales Department in New York at (212) 967-8800 or (800) 322-8755.

You can find Chelsea House on the World Wide Web at http://www.infobaselearning.com

Text design by Erika K. Arroyo
Cover design by Alicia Post
Composition by EJB Publishing Services
Cover printed by Yurchak Printing, Landisville, Pa.
Book printed and bound by Yurchak Printing, Landisville, Pa.

Printed in the United States of America

This book is printed on acid-free paper.

All links and Web addresses were checked and verified to be correct at the time of publication. Because of the dynamic nature of the Web, some addresses and links may have changed since publication and may no longer be valid.

Contents

A Veiled Mystery

John Lloyd Stephens stopped and wiped his sweaty brow. The hot Mexican sun beat down through the jungle trees, sapping the strength of the American at the head of a small caravan. The air was heavy and moist, requiring members of the group to exert themselves harder for each step they took, for each swing of the machete, for each breath. Despite the effort required, the group slowly moved forward through the dense undergrowth of the Mexican jungle. Mosquitoes, flies, and a seemingly endless supply and variety of insects hovered around each man. Still, the group pressed on. After making headway into the brush, the leader called for a halt. It was time to take a break. As each member of the team quickly grasped a canteen and quenched his greedy thirst, the leader stood quietly in the shade of a large tree and pondered their progress. He and the others had already seen pyramids and stood in buildings that had been built over 1,000 years earlier. Despite their success, Stephens wanted to see as many other sites as he could. The jungle growth hid the objects they sought, but somehow the effort only increased their desire to see the lost cities. Each branch or vine cut away might reveal a new stone carving, an archway, or steps—any of which might be the beginning of a new and exciting place to explore.

Just 35 years old, John Lloyd Stephens had already experienced life as few in his time could have imagined. However, Stephens was an unlikely explorer. Born in 1805 in New Jersey and raised in Massachusetts, he attended Columbia College before completing law school at the University of Connecticut in 1823. Stephens seemed more interested in traveling than in practicing law. He took two extended trips abroad, one in 1835 and another in 1836. On these trips, he visited Europe, including Italy, Greece, and Turkey, and Jerusalem. He wrote letters describing his trips, which he later published as books. These publications had earned him recognition as an author and traveler.

Stephens shifted slightly, trying to get as much relief as possible from the sun by stepping all the way into the shade of a large tree. Large sweat stains marked wide arcs on his shirt under his armpits and spread down his chest and back. His ears, cheeks, nose, and the skin exposed on his arms were all tan. Insects buzzed all around his body, especially around his face and hands, which bore the marks of previous bites and stings. The humidity was both high and constant, the group feeling it from the time they awoke each morning, throughout the heat of the day, until after dark, when each drifted off to sleep. Stephens looked at his boots. They were covered with mud and the leather was wet, soaked all the way through. His feet were wet, and he knew that when he removed his boots and socks in camp that night, as he did each night, his feet would be white and wrinkled from the daylong contact with moisture. His clothes—pants and shirt, even his boots—were slightly moldy from the constant exposure to water. The rain and humidity created a constant state of moistness that gave one the sense things were never really dry.

Despite the hardships, Stephens relished every moment. This was the kind of trip he had always wanted to take; this was the kind of adventure he had longed for. Indeed, the first elements for this trip began to fall into place years before Stephens even knew he wanted to travel. Were it not for a continuing sore throat that plagued him, he might never have taken a trip out of the United States. A sympathetic physician advised him that sea travel might ease his throat pain. Stephens followed his advice, traveling abroad. On his travels, he gained an appreciation for other cultures, admiring their architecture and art.

During one of his trips, Stephens met a young English artist named Frederick Catherwood. This acquaintance proved fortunate, as the two would later take an unforgettable trip together, a trip that illuminated the Maya to the world for the first time. In his various travels, Stephens had heard stories of lost cities filled with temples and pyramids in the jungles of Central America. The young traveler began to dream of exploring these sites himself. All known literature on the region at the time described the ruins as remote, difficult to find, and virtually impossible

In the late seventeenth century, there was little information on the Maya in Middle America. John Lloyd Stephens, an adventurous American, was the first English-speaking explorer to see ancient Maya sites. His friend, Frederick Catherwood, documented these expeditions with drawings (*above*).

to reach. Stephens read works by the early Spanish explorers and missionaries to the region, as well as those written by others who had visited the region. There was little written on the area, and much of it was incomplete. Many did not believe the cities actually existed, and if they did exist, they thought the stories about them were probably exaggerated and inaccurate. Others believed they existed, but no one knew who had built them. All of the stories deepened the mystery about the lost and deserted cities in the jungle.

Stephens had managed to secure an appointment as minister to Central America from President Martin Van Buren. Such a post guaranteed safe passage to the places Stephens wanted to explore. Now Stephens could travel into the jungles of Central America, and he could do so legally.

Importantly, he could also take Frederick Catherwood with him to help document what they found. When they made their expedition, Stephens and Catherwood became the first English-speaking travelers to visit and see the ancient Maya sites.

FREDERICK CATHERWOOD

Frederick Catherwood was an English architect and artist who accompanied Stephens on this trip. Catherwood was already an accomplished artist who had traveled widely prior to this trek with Stephens. The artist planned to illustrate Stephens's book detailing the Maya ruins they were exploring. Forty years old at the time of the expedition, Catherwood did not know it when the expedition started, but his work would become the first visual record of the amazing Maya accomplishments for the Western world. Equally important, his knowledge of architecture in North Africa and the Middle East helped dispel the notion that some people other than the Maya built the Maya cities. Catherwood recognized the Maya pyramids, palaces, temples, and other buildings to be unique, unlike those built by civilizations that some wrongly assumed might have built the structures in Central America—civilizations such as the ancient Egyptians, Carthaginians, and Phoenicians.

Catherwood's artwork captured the visual essence of the Maya ruins, bringing them to life for many around the world who would never have the opportunity to travel there and see the ruins themselves. For others, the artwork served as inspiration to study the ancient people, appreciate their accomplishments, decipher their hieroglyphs, and record their history. Even today, Catherwood's illustrations are vivid reminders of Maya greatness when its civilization was at its height.

To accomplish his task, Catherwood used a primitive camera device, called a camera lucida, to help him make accurate drawings of the Maya ruins. *Camera lucida* in Latin literally means a chamber or room with light. The portable device, unlike other similar devices available at the time, did not require special lighting because no image is projected by the apparatus. Instead, the artist uses a mirror, placed at a 45 degree angle, to look at the drawing surface. In so doing, the artist sees both the drawing surface and the object or scene being drawn at the same time. Although the tools he used were simple, Catherwood's drawings accurately depicted the Maya ruins.

UNCOVERING THE RUINS

Stephens swatted a mosquito from his wrist. He remembered how, just a few months before, he and Catherwood left from New York for Belize. Sailing down the coast, it took them a month to reach Belize. From there, they traveled by horse and mule while local Indians slowly cleared the path before them, using machetes. Bit by bit, the group made its way through the dense jungle, weathering an earthquake along the way. Locals did not always receive them kindly, but the group persevered. The first site they came upon was in Honduras, the city of Copán. The first remains the ambassador had seen there were carved columns. Stephens remembered the excitement he felt that day. Seeing the detail of the artwork, as he later wrote in his *Incidents of Travel in Central America, Chiapas, and Yucatán*, convinced him "that the people who once occupied the Continent of America were not savages." The pyramids, palaces, and temples he had seen since that first day in Copán further proved that it had been an advanced civilization that had constructed such monuments and massive works of architecture.

After spending some time in Copán drawing and exploring the ruins, Stephens and the others continued their survey of the region, visiting site after site of ancient Maya ruins. Each day, the group hacked their way through a seemingly endless array of vines, shrubs, and trees as they made their way to the deserted cities. Upon arriving at a set of ruins, they faced the same overgrowth of vegetation, as well as debris from the buildings. In addition, the heat, humidity, and bugs were constantly part of the experience. The group fought their way to each site and then struggled to maneuver within each site. The work was exhausting, draining each member of the team of his strength. But still they pressed on, eager to discover a new site, anxious to set foot in another deserted city. The lure of the unknown, the chance to explore and explain a mystery, had spurred them on.

Stephens laughed to himself when he thought of what the trip had cost him. True, the hardships were almost unimaginable. But the rugged and loyal Indian laborers who toiled tirelessly each worked for a mere 18 cents a day! More amazingly, Stephens had purchased the entire ruins at Copán from a local chieftain. The traveler could hardly believe that he had bought one of the greatest cities of the Maya civilization for just $50!

Now, in late May 1840, Stephens and the others were camped at Palenque, the last Maya site they planned to see before returning to civilization. The trip had exhausted them all. Biting *garrapatas*, or ticks, afflicted the men day and night. Mosquitoes, carrying the threat of disease, constantly buzzed around them. The constant heat and humidity fatigued the men. At Palenque, the group also weathered rain and flooding.

Despite the hardships, the group continued to go about their work. They made a raised platform for Catherwood, enabling him to stand above the growth and see the ruins more clearly. From his scaffolding, the artist generated a set of remarkable illustrations that captured the images of the Maya ruins. The artist endured insect bites and humidity as he dutifully stood on his platform hour after hour each day and drew Palenque's ruins. While he drew pictures, Stephens and the others counted and took measurements of the pillars, pyramids, temples, and other Maya structures.

The group weathered bugs, rain, and the heat to complete their survey of the ruins of Palenque. Rainstorms made it nearly impossible to remain, and the group had to move their camp to avoid local flooding. Finally, after 10 days, Catherwood completed his last drawing, and the group prepared to leave their temporary lodging in the swampy ruins. Stephens later wrote in his *Incidents of Travel in Central America, Chiapas, and Yucatán*, that on Saturday, June 1, 1840, "like rats leaving a sinking ship, we broke up and left the ruins." Returning to the coast and to the comforts of civilization, Stephens and Catherwood ended the trip that alerted the world to the Maya.

A VEIL OF MYSTERY

Who built these massive buildings? How did these people live? John Lloyd Stephens asked these kinds of questions. Stephens also published two books describing his trek into the Central American jungles and his discoveries of the Maya ruins. For his work, Stephens is often called the "father of Maya archaeology." More than 160 years have passed since John Lloyd Stephens, Frederick Catherwood, and their caravan braved the heat, humidity, and bugs and uncovered vines and branches to reveal Maya buildings. Since the Stephens expedition, researchers, historians, and archaeologists have devoted entire careers to learning more about the Maya. With each passing decade, more is discovered and understood about this great Mesoamerican civilization. We now know that the Maya domesticated corn, built immense buildings with no metal tools, constructed large cities while living in the rural hinterland, conceived complex mathematics, and studied the heavens in ways that Western civilization would not until centuries later.

Although Stephens and Catherwood did not know it, their work opened the door to continual interest and study of the Maya. As historian Sylvanus Griswold Morley points out, "Stephens' writings were chiefly responsible for bringing the great cities of Maya civilization to the attention of the outside world." Morley also notes that after Stephens published his works, "the period of the modern exploration" of the Maya region began. The lure of the unknown attracted Stephens to travel to remote settings to see ruins up close and in person. As he later wrote in his *Incidents of Travel in Yucatán*:

Starting in Belize, Stephens and his exploration team headed inland in search of ancient Maya ruins. Hacking their way through dense, hot jungle, they were plagued by mosquitoes and other bugs but were able to discover some previously unknown ancient sites, all of which were documented by Catherwood (*above*).

We had seen, abandoned and in ruins, the same buildings which the Spaniards saw entire and inhabited, by Indians, and we had identified them without question as the works of the same people who created the great ruined cities over which, when we began our journey, hung a veil of seemingly impenetrable mystery. At that time, we believed the discovery and comparison of these remains to be the surest, if not the only means, of removing this veil.

Since Stephens's expedition, researchers have continued to discover and compare the remains of the Maya civilization. From their research, the world has learned many things about the Maya civilization, which first appeared as long as 4,000 years ago but rose to its peak between A.D. 200 and 900. Then, as suddenly as they had arisen, the Maya cities emptied. Over time, the deserted urban centers were taken over by the dense vegetation of the ever-encroaching jungle. The Maya culture survived intact until the Spanish arrived in the sixteenth century. The Spanish conquerors imposed uniformity and brought their religious customs, language, and other cultural components wherever they went. Despite the influx of Spanish culture, the Maya still maintained much of their cultural identity.

The Maya culture boasted many achievements that rivaled and even surpassed other ancient civilizations. The Maya developed a calendar that kept track of both sacred and government events. They were actively engaged in trade throughout the region, and their location allowed them to thrive as traders. The Maya economy included artisans and merchants, as well as farmers. As part of their rituals, the ancient Maya also played a ball game that sometimes cost the losing team their lives. Maya cities included large pyramids made of stone, as well as sites that were used for public and religious ceremonies, including human sacrifices.

The Maya developed a highly sophisticated writing system using hieroglyphs, or picture words. They carved hieroglyphs on stone pillars, buildings, and walls. They also painted their writing on paper made from bark or animal skin, bone, wood, jade, and even shells. The Maya also studied the skies, enabling them to recognize the patterns of movement of the planets and stars. To accomplish this, the Maya built observatories made of stone, and some of their temples were positioned so that their location would be exactly aligned to some astronomical event such as the summer solstice or the spring equinox. The Maya precisely traced and predicted the positions of Mars and Venus in the sky. They also recognized the phases of the moon and accurately predicted both solar and lunar eclipses.

Stephens did not live to realize his dreams of understanding the Maya civilization. Indeed, he never returned to the Maya ruins. In 1852, suffering from the effects of malaria or some other ailment he contracted in Panama, John Lloyd Stephens died at the age of 47. Frederick Catherwood died just two years later, on September 20, 1854, while traveling to the United States from Liverpool, England. The artist and many others were killed when the steamer they were on, the *Artic*, was accidentally struck and sunk by a French ship.

In spite of their deaths, the work of Stephens and Catherwood laid the foundation for the continued uncovering of the deserted Maya cities. The mystery of the ruins had excited and attracted them to Central America. In the more than 160 years since, the ruins continue to draw others to Central America to explore and understand the civilization that built massive cities in the jungle. And in that time, researchers have shed more light on the mysteries of the Maya.

Early Maya

The Maya lived and flourished in a place scholars call Mesoamerica, which is a term describing a geographical location as well as a collection of related cultures. Geographically, Mesoamerica is in Central America. In rough terms, Mesoamerica stretches from Costa Rica to the desert north of the Valley of Mexico, including what is now western Honduras and all of the Yucatán Peninsula. Today, this area and some of the nearby countries are often called Middle America. When historians use the term *Mesoamerica*, they are usually referring to the people, culture, and events that lived, thrived, and occurred in this region before the Spanish arrived in 1521. This period dates back to the arrival of humans in the region, perhaps as early as 21,000 B.C.

Scholars divide the history of human events into four different periods. These divisions allow researchers to gain a deeper understanding of the people and their culture as they study ruins and artifacts. These four divisions are the Archaic Period (about 20,000 to 2500 B.C.), the Preclassic Period (about 2500 B.C. to A.D. 250), the Classic Period (about A.D. 250 to 900), and the Postclassic Period (A.D. 900 to the 1500s and the arrival of the Spanish).

WHO WERE THE MAYA?

Many scholars believe that the Maya descended from individuals who crossed the Bering Strait at least 20,000 years ago. These hunter-gatherers lived a nomadic lifestyle, moving from one place to the next in pursuit of food. The earliest settlements in Mexico appeared sometime between 5000 and 1500 B.C., during the Archaic Period. These early settlements included the use of stone tools, the creation and use of pottery, and the cultivation of maize, or corn. The earliest civilization in the region, which rose up during the Preclassic Period, was that of the Olmec, who settled along the Gulf coast. Little survives of this civilization, leaving scholars with not much of an understanding of them.

Perhaps the most well-known of the Mesoamerican civilizations is that of the Maya. Scholars identify the beginning of Maya history in the Yucatán around 2600 B.C., or the end of the Archaic Period. The Maya advanced and flourished beginning about A.D. 250 in what is now northern Belize, El Salvador, western Honduras, Guatemala, and southern Mexico. The Maya inherited knowledge from the Olmec and added their own creative skills to develop their own calendars and mathematical and writing systems. In addition, the Maya studied the sun, the moon, and Venus, recording and accurately predicting the patterns and cycles of these heavenly bodies. Moreover, this civilization raised up enormous and impressive stone structures—palaces, ball courts, observatories, and pyramids. Incredibly, they built these buildings without metal tools! Other architectural achievements include reservoirs for storing water during the dry months.

The Maya also took advantage of their location, acting as merchant traders in the region. Their trade routes followed paths on land and on the sea, extending throughout Central America, passing through tropical jungles, and following along the coast. In agriculture, the Maya cleared trees and planted sustainable crops.

In short, the Maya developed their civilization into an advanced culture, accomplishing architectural feats, perfecting mathematical and calendar systems, and creating a written language. Each of these accomplishments was without parallel in other civilizations of the New World until much later. Some of these achievements predated those same advancements in the Western world. The Maya were indeed an advanced society with great accomplishments.

Due to their location, not much is known about the earliest Maya. Other than stone, metal, or other hard materials, few artifacts have survived due to the tropical climates in which the Maya lived. Despite the difficulties, scholars know that early Maya, or peoples closely related to them, first settled near the Mexican border, on the Pacific coast of modern-day

Guatemala. The different groups spoke different dialects and, in some cases, different Mayan languages altogether.

At the height of the Maya civilization, there may have been as many as 2 million people, most of whom lived in what is now Guatemala. The civilization was centered in more than 50 cities in Mesoamerica. Most of the population lived around and near the cities, which served more as their religious and ceremonial sites than dwelling places. The great cities in the south declined around A.D. 900, but the Maya cities in the Yucatán (i.e., Chichén Itzá, Uxmal, and Mayapán) continued to flourish until the arrival and conquest of the Spanish in the early sixteenth century. The Spanish imposed their rule and Roman Catholicism on most of the remaining Maya. Descendants of the Maya live today in Belize, Guatemala, and southern Mexico.

DAILY LIFE

Much of what scholars know about Maya living in the Classic Period comes from the writings of Bishop Diego de Landa, who first encountered the Indians in 1549. Although most of the city-states no longer had organized ruling classes, many aspects of the culture and daily life were still intact. Landa observed and recorded many of these traits, giving us a valuable record of ancient Maya life.

Most Maya were bowlegged, probably due to the fashion in which mothers carried their young with one leg on each side of them. Many were cross-eyed since they believed it to be beautiful and encouraged this trait by attaching an object to hang down between the eyes of infants. The Maya also tied a board onto the forehead and back side of the head of their babies, causing their heads to be flat. The Maya also pierced the ears of their young. Most wore tattoos but did not tattoo themselves until after marriage.

Maya men did not wear beards. The few that did sported coarse-whiskered beards. Men and women wore little clothing, mostly a loincloth, which they decorated with feathers, and a long square wrap that they tied to their shoulders. They also wore sandals, made of deer hide and hemp (a tough plant fiber). The men bathed often and in the open, with no coverings. Landa describes men painting their bodies red, but the ancient glyphs do not indicate whether this was a practice in the Classic Period.

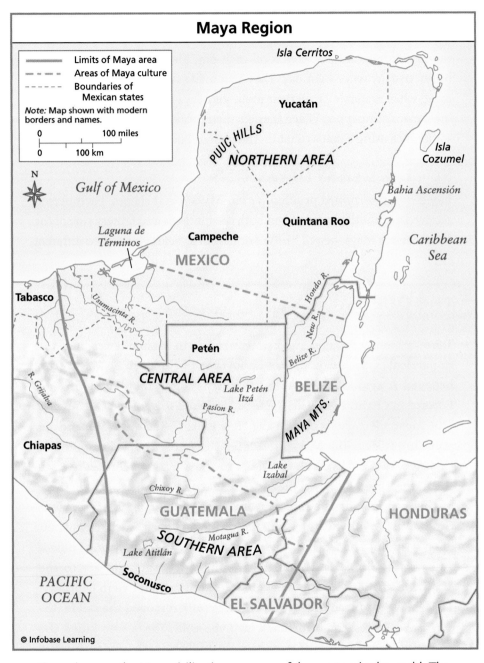

Maya Region

Legend:
- Limits of Maya area
- Areas of Maya culture
- Boundaries of Mexican states

Note: Map shown with modern borders and names.

0 — 100 miles
0 — 100 km

N

Isla Cerritos

Yucatán

PUUC HILLS

NORTHERN AREA

Isla Cozumel

Gulf of Mexico

Bahía Ascensión

Laguna de Términos

Campeche

Quintana Roo

Caribbean Sea

MEXICO

Tabasco

Usumacinta R.

Hondo R.

New R.

Petén

Belize R.

CENTRAL AREA

Lake Petén Itzá

BELIZE

R. Grijalva

Pasíon R.

MAYA MTS.

Chiapas

Lake Izabal

Chixoy R.

GUATEMALA

HONDURAS

Motagua R.

SOUTHERN AREA

Lake Atitlán

Soconusco

PACIFIC OCEAN

EL SALVADOR

© Infobase Learning

Centuries ago, the Maya civilization was one of the greatest in the world. The Maya made remarkable advances in math, science, and architecture. They occupied Mesoamerica, a region that encompasses modern-day Central American countries such as Guatemala, Belize, and Honduras.

Men and women performed their roles within society. The men hunted game in the forest and planted, weeded, and harvested the crops. Women raised children and prepared food each day. They ground corn to make bread, usually twice each day. They also made stews with vegetables and meat, when available. In all their food, the Maya added spices and seasonings, especially pepper. When they ate their meals, they did so on the floor, sometimes using a mat as a table. The men did not eat with the women.

SOCIAL CLASS DIVISIONS

Bloodlines determined position within Maya social classes. Each person received an inherited name from both the mother's and father's side of the family. Every Maya viewed himself or herself as belonging to two different

THE QUETZAL

There are many colorful and beautiful birds in Mesoamerica, but one in particular, the quetzal, was important to the ancient Maya, who believed it symbolized life and fertility. Roger Tory Peterson and Edward L. Chalif, in *A Field Guide to Mexican Birds*, called the quetzal "the most spectacular bird in the New World." The quetzal is indeed stunning to see. The Maya, and later the Aztec, viewed the bird as their most sacred symbol. *Kukulkán* to the Maya and *Quetzalcoatl* to the Aztec, the god's name meant "the feathered serpent." Depictions of this god include the long tail feathers of the quetzal. In ancient times, only royalty were permitted to include such feathers in their dress. Wearing the feathers of the quetzal was an expression of power and wealth. Similarly, the bird symbolized freedom and life to the Maya, who believed a quetzal would die rather than live in captivity. Thus, Maya captured the birds alive, carefully removed the tail feathers, and released the birds back into the wild. Those who killed the beautiful birds faced stiff penalties, including death, giving further evidence of how sacred and important the birds were to the Maya.

The word *quetzal* means "tail feathers." On the male of the species, the tail feathers are difficult to miss. The adult quetzal is groups: matrilineal and patrilineal. The patrilineal group was made up of relatives and descendants of the father (or patriarch), whereas the matrilineal group was made up of relatives and descendants of the mother (or matriarch). Property inheritance was restricted and could be passed only through the father.

Bonds within a patrilineal group were strong. Members of the group shared ownership of family land, which helped strengthen the family ties. Also, if a member of the patrilineal group was enslaved to pay a debt or due to a crime, then other members of the group paid the debt. However, in terms of prestige, both sides of the family tree mattered. A Maya man who could trace his lineage to a noble through both the matrilineal and patrilineal groups was held in high regard. In fact, the Maya word for

approximately 14 inches (35.5 centimeters) long, and the male sports tail feathers that can reach a length of 40 inches (1 meter). The breast and most of the body is a bright crimson, with white feathers near its feet. The head and upper plumage are a glittering green. The two to three tail feathers are an iridescent green, shifting from gold to green to blue, and their length helps make the bird distinctive. The female lacks the long tail feathers, and her gray-green plumage is not as brightly colored as the male.

Quetzals eat insects and small animals such as lizards or frogs. However, the birds primarily eat fruit and especially favor wild avocados. They live in dense, cloud-covered forests at altitudes ranging from 4,000 to 10,500 feet (1,219 to 3,200 m). With small numbers and encroaching development threatening their habitat, efforts have been made to protect this magnificent bird. Reserves offering protection have been established in the highlands of Guatemala and near El Triunfo, Chiapas (Mexico). Designed to protect the rain forest and its wildlife, these preserves offer hope for this rare and amazing bird. Otherwise, the quetzal, revered by the Maya, faces extinction.

noble, *almehen*, literally means a man whose bloodline can be read on both sides. In other words, the Maya viewed others as noble if they were descended from nobility on both sides of the family. All those holding government positions, wealthy merchants, landowners, and priests were members of the nobility class. Scribes, who received education in order to read and write, also held a place within the nobility.

The class divisions were emphasized in the jobs people performed, the dress they wore, and the architecture of the cities in which they lived. The more basic and unskilled the task one performed, the lower the class. The brighter and fancier the clothing one wore, the higher the class. The closer one lived to the city center, the higher the class. The king, along with his family and servants, and the nobility lived near the greatest and most prominent temple compound in the center of the city. Thus, the temple and related buildings usually formed the center, with the king and other nobles living nearby, usually in large, impressive structures. The lower the rank, the farther out from the center one lived, usually in dwellings that were more modest. Likewise, the sizes of homes farther out from the temple square were smaller.

SCRIBES

Those within Maya society who painted and drew for the ruler were known as scribes. The Maya words for these individuals literally meant "scribe" and "painter." Priests watched for those who had an aptitude for drawing or painting. The priests chose those who showed promise to begin training to develop their gift. The chosen ones underwent schooling to learn the basics of the Maya culture and language. After studying the basics, scribes and painters then dedicated themselves to learning the intricacies of a specialized field, such as astronomy, history, mathematics, medicine, etc.

Following several years of serving as apprentices, scribes graduated to a level of mastery that enabled them to work as professionals within their specialized field of study. To pursue their profession, scribes and painters relocated to urban centers that needed their skills. A religious scribe lived near a temple, whereas a scribe well versed in history would live and work near a ruling family.

Once employed, a scribe or painter dedicated all of his time to working on the codices needed. Scholars believe that it took several scribes or painters working several days to complete a single codex. Using a cactus thorn or a small bone splinter, the scribe used black ink, made of coal, to outline each figure. Then, using a paintbrush made of animal hair, the scribe completed the picture with the appropriate colors. Since many of these images include several colors, it took time and concentration to paint a single image. After completing his tedious assignment without recognition, the scribe's individual contribution would be included with the work of other scribes to form a completed project. Rooms set aside for storing the completed codices were located within the temple, palace, or building within which the scribes worked. The meticulous workers rarely left the buildings in which they anonymously toiled for the benefit of rulers and priests.

Scholars believe that the colors in a codex are not included for decorative or artistic purposes. Instead, each color and even shades of colors are believed to be symbolic. Each color represented a particular deity or characteristic to the Maya. Thus, each picture represented the being or scene depicted but also represented ideas based on the colors included in the portrayal.

Scribes performed the elite function of reading and writing in a culture where few could read and write. Socially, scribes were members of the nobility, and some believed they were related to members of the ruling class, sometimes even the king. They fulfilled an important task by commemorating the accomplishments of a king. This written record, whether written on bark, carved in stone, or painted on stucco, served as a reminder to all of the king's power and prestige. Other kinds of text were less formal, such as hieroglyphs found on clay pots.

Recent scholarship indicates that some of these texts were intended to be read aloud to groups of people. Kevin Johnston, an anthropologist at Ohio State University, in a *National Geographic* online article, says that writing in Maya society "was a political tool of persuasion and authority. Scribes were deliberately targeted in warfare to silence the king's mouthpiece, which would compromise his power and reveal his vulnerability." Johnston became interested in the fate of scribes captured in warfare after observing murals that depicted scribes with broken or amputated fingers before being executed. Johnston believes the victorious kings took steps to ensure scribes appropriately recorded their accomplishments. Since scribes were likely related to the king, a captured scribe was likely to hold loyalties to the vanquished, not the conquering, hero.

SLAVES

Maya society included slaves. Most were those captured in war. Usually, only the most noble and prominent captives were held for ritualistic sacrifices. All other, less-wealthy captives faced a life of slavery. Other slaves included those working off a sentence, such as for theft. Still others were slaves simply because they were too poor to survive without being sold or even selling themselves into slavery. The Maya also engaged in slave trading as part of their immense trading network throughout Mesoamerica. Most slaves faced a lifetime of servitude, with no chance of gaining freedom. Children born into slavery remained slaves. Freedom could be purchased, but few could afford that luxury.

To differentiate them from free Maya men, male slaves sported a short haircut and dressed in tattered clothing. Male slaves performed manual labor for merchants, served as fishermen, and functioned as laborers in almost any kind of unskilled and tedious task that needed doing. In the same way, the Maya used female slaves to perform manual tasks. Female slaves performed the traditional Maya female work roles: they dyed cloth, ground maize, and drew water for their masters.

MAYA LAW AND PUNISHMENT

Religious beliefs greatly influenced Maya law. The Maya did not believe that things happened by accident. Rather, all occurrences took place as the fulfillment of a design or patterns. The stars held the key to understanding these patterns. Since no action was an accident, there was no such thing as an accident in the eyes of the law. Those accused of accidentally causing damage or death were treated as if the damage or death were done on purpose. Religious belief viewed the accused as chosen by a god or the gods to suffer this fate. Thus, the accused was forced to repay for damages with money or repay a life lost with a life. For poor Maya who lacked money or wealthy relatives, the only way to repay damages was to enter slavery until the debt was paid to the victim's family.

Punishment for crimes was both harsh and immediate. Lawbreakers received whippings that left visible marks, to announce their shame and to serve as a warning to others. Each city-state had councils of judges to handle criminal cases. These councils would inquire of the priests at local temples to help determine the verdict. Again, the Maya believed that all actions could be explained by reading the stars, so the judges simply

This social pyramid represents the hierarchy of Maya society, with the king at the top and the slaves and servants at the lowest level. If one were a member of a specific social class, it would be apparent in his or her dress, location of his or her home, and occupation.

asked the priests what the stars said about a specific situation. Judges dispatched runners to the temple. Once a runner returned with the verdict, which was written on an obsidian block, the judges imposed the sentence immediately. A guilty verdict usually meant payment or slavery, torture, or death. A public and central platform served as the stage for carrying out verdicts of torture and death.

Bishop Diego de Landa observed Maya justice dispensed and later wrote about it. The sentence for murder was death. Officials placed a murderer in stocks on the platform. Relatives of the victim then killed the accused. Even killing an animal for no apparent or justifiable reason was cause for punishment in Maya society. Such a crime was similar to murder, although the accused faced severe punishment rather than death.

Maya hunters showed respect for the animals they hunted and killed for food. Hunters believed they needed to make atonement or compensation for the killing. In order to do this, Maya hunters drew blood from their tongue or penis and sprinkled the blood on the animal as sign of respect.

The Maya severely punished other crimes, too. Maya houses did not have doors, meaning anyone could enter at any time. To alert them that someone entered, the Maya hung bell strings in the entryway. Due to the lack of doors, they considered stealing a serious offense. For their crimes, thieves faced either slavery or repaying the cost of the theft. Those forced into slavery served until full repayment had been made. Wealthy criminals or those with wealthy relatives could pay off the price of reimbursement.

The ancient Maya treated adultery as another serious offense worthy of death, at least for the man. Women caught in adultery were allowed to live a life of disgrace following the incident after being punished. However, a man caught in adultery faced humiliation, torture, and then death. Once seized, the adulterer's hands and feet were tied. Then, the offender was hauled before the council of judges. After hearing the case, the judges pronounced guilt and handed the man over to the husband, who was allowed to kill the accused. The husband carried out the death sentence by dropping a large stone onto the head of the accused. Such was the way of Maya justice.

It is important to note that the Maya did not imprison any lawbreakers. Instead, the offender received swift and harsh punishment for his or her crime. Imprisonment was reserved for captives seized in war. The Maya treated their captives with respect and did not mistreat them while in captivity. They held captives for only one purpose: They served as human sacrifices on special days. When a key festival or ritual anniversary arrived, the captives faced torture and death at the hands of their enemies. The Maya performed these ritualistic tortures and killings in order to honor their gods. Each city-state sought captives from rival city-states in order to celebrate religious festivals and rituals of human sacrifice.

The Maya Economy

Historians believe that the first humans to migrate to the Americas did so at least 20,000 years ago. These early wanderers crossed the land bridge that then extended over what is now the Bering Strait. These nomads wandered south and east onto the North American continent, reaching the Central American isthmus about 13,000 years ago. While the Ice Age lasted, these transplants continued to live as they had in Asia, hunting large mammals such as mammoths and mastodons. However, the climate began to warm and the ice caps began to melt. The land bridge between Asia and North America disappeared. Changes to the climate also led to the extinction of the large Ice Age mammals. Humans started hunting smaller game and gathering vegetation to complete their changing diet. As natives looked increasingly to crops for food, the need to settle and raise a crop altered lifestyles from a nomadic way of life to a settled one.

The Maya primarily depended upon three crops for sustenance: maize, squash, and beans. Researchers believe that maize, or corn, developed from a grass and grew wild until humans intentionally cultivated it as a crop.

MAIZE

It is difficult to overstate the importance of Indian corn to agriculture within the New World prior to Columbus. The cultivation of corn supplied natives throughout North and South America with the means to feed large numbers of people, enabling civilizations such as the Maya to collect the necessary workforce to construct massive temples and large urban centers.

Plant biologists disagree as to where corn originated. There is strong evidence suggesting humans first cultivated maize in the highlands of what is now Peru. Others believe the key crop was first grown in modern-day western Guatemala. Historians often date the first cultivation of corn around 2500 B.C. Regardless of its origin, maize quickly spread throughout the Americas as the basic food for most humans and the chief staple for Mesoamerican civilizations.

Maya agricultural practices that predate the Classic Period persist to this day. These practices include the clearing of trees, burning the cleared vegetation and remaining brush, followed by the planting of crops in the now rich topsoil. After planting and harvesting in a place for a few years and depleting the soil, the Maya repeated the process elsewhere in order to increase crop production. These techniques worked well in the jungles in particular. The climate and conditions enable the land to handle this kind of treatment. In many respects, this was the only effective approach for ancient peoples living in the rain forests of Mesoamerica. The land in this region has shallow soil covering limestone. Bishop Diego de Landa, in his *Account of the Affairs of Yucatán*, claimed to "have never seen a country with so little soil as Yucatán, for the whole land is made of limestone." He went on to describe the richness of the rocky soil. In addition, the region is densely covered with trees, and the natives there lacked large draft animals one might expect for a people relying on agriculture as the primary food source.

Those living in Maya lands have used this slash-and-burn technique for centuries. Since the soil is rocky and relatively shallow, those living in the rain forests with little access to modern technologies have little choice but to continue the practice. The nature of the soil makes modern equipment ineffective. According to historian Sylvanus Griswold Morley, "the Yucatán Maya word for cornfield is col, and all the Maya Languages have similar words for it." Morley goes on to state, "Making the cornfield is the most important single activity for Maya men today, as it was in ancient times." The centrality of corn to the Maya diet highlights the importance of the crop to their culture.

Even the tools have changed little since the Classic Period. Today's ancestors wielded a stone ax for clearing trees; a fire-hardened, pointed

The Maya developed agricultural techniques that allowed them to maximize their main crops of corn, beans, and squash. Chocolate was also frequently consumed and used in religious ceremonies to calm people before they were sacrificed to the Sovereign Plumed Serpent God (*above*).

stick for planting; and a bag to carry the seed corn. Today's maize farmer carries a steel ax, along with a steel machete. In addition, he also has the pointed planting stick, but it is tipped with iron to aid in planting. Like his ancestors, he still carries a bag with seed corn. The tools are more modern, but the techniques are virtually unaltered. Scholars believe that the modern Maya still plant corn using the same techniques their ancestors used hundreds of years ago. Landa described the process:

> They plant in many places, so that if one fails the others will suffice. In cultivating the land, they do nothing more than clear the brush, and burn it in order to sow it afterward, and from the middle of January to April, they work it and when the rains come they plant it, which they do by carrying a small sack on the shoulders, and with a pointed stick, they make a hole in the ground, dropping in it five or six grains, covering them with the same stick. And when it rains, it is marvelous to see how it grows.

Landa's description is almost identical to current methods in the region, meaning the Maya continue to farm in the same ways they did more than 400 years ago. In addition, researchers believe that the techniques Landa observed were in place during the Classic Period, which ended in A.D. 900.

Farmers burned the cleared brush on the day selected by the priests, who used the calendars to determine the proper day for the task. Their reliance on corn and other planted crops demonstrates the need for a reliable calendar for planting dates. Without an accurate calendar, farmers did not know when to plant their crops.

One practice unique to Mesoamerican corn farming is that of bending the stalks. This is done when the corn is ripe. The stalks are bent just below the ear, causing them to harden in this position. Mesoamerican corn stalks are very tall, reaching heights of nearly 15 feet (4.6 m). Modern Maya claim that doing this to the corn stalks prevents rain from entering the ears, thereby preventing mold. Today, only modern Maya practice this technique in the production of corn.

BEANS, SQUASH, AND OTHER MAYA CROPS

Beans are second only to maize in the Maya diet. Black beans and another bean that is multicolored were both raised and eaten by the ancient Maya.

Under current agricultural practices, farmers place bean seeds in the same planting hole as the corn seeds. Thus, beans and corn grow from the same hole, limiting the amount of weeding and other maintenance work necessary for raising and harvesting a crop. The downside to this approach is that a local condition that damages one crop is likely to damage the other as well.

The Maya also raised other crops. According to Landa, they had "many kinds of gourds, some of which have seeds that may be used for making stews while some are eaten grilled and boiled and others are made into vessels." The Maya also raised melons, roots, and other vegetables to supplement their diet. In addition to growing maize, squash, and beans for food, the Maya also raised an important crop for the nobility and for trade: cacao.

MAYA HUNTING

The Maya also hunted animals and birds to supplement their largely agricultural diet. Hunters used traps and snares to catch deer. In addition, hunters sought peccaries (small, piglike animals), rabbits, squirrels, and a variety of rodents. Maya hunters used a blowpipe, which was basically a blow gun. A hunter used the blowpipe to launch small clay pellets at prey. Skilled hunters could do this with enough velocity to hit and kill their target.

The Maya also tamed animals, some for food, others for companionship. They raised various birds, especially chickens, for food and also used the feathers for clothing decorations. They even managed to tame deer by nursing them with other animals. Maya living along the coast enjoyed fresh fish, turtles, and even manatees.

THE IMPORTANCE OF MAIZE

The growing season in the Yucatán is reasonably short. Morley observed and studied the techniques of modern Maya farmers, who use the same methods as their ancient ancestors. Morley estimates that a Maya farmer need only invest about 76 days of work to raise enough corn for his family and livestock. If the same farmer does not also raise livestock, the amount of work required to provide food for the family for the year drops to only 48 days. How can this be? The application of slash-and-burn techniques to prepare a field, long practiced by the Maya, takes less time than other

CHOCOLATE!

Chocolate today is usually considered a sweet candy. However, chocolate has a rich history dating back to ancient times when the Maya first processed and drank chocolate. For the Maya, chocolate was not simply a tasty treat. Instead, it played a vital part in their religious rituals. The ancient Maya drank chocolate at religious events and royal celebrations. Cacao ("cocoa" in English) seeds, a prized possession and the currency of the Maya, were often presented as offerings to the gods during religious ceremonies. They also planted cacao trees in their family plots. During the Classic Period, the Maya learned how to process the cacao beans for use as a drink. After harvesting the pods, the Maya allowed the beans within the pods to ferment and dry. Then, they removed the seeds and roasted them over a fire. They ground the roasted seeds into a paste, and then mixed the paste with water, chili pepper, ground corn, and honey. The drink was then poured back and forth between two containers, causing it to froth and giving it a foam head. The resulting drink tasted bitter, since the Maya did not have access to sweeteners other than honey. They enjoyed it both as a hot and a cold drink.

Scholars believe that the Spanish coined the word *chocolate*, combining the Maya word for "cacao" (*chocol*) and the Aztec word for "water" (*atl*), resulting in *chocoatl*, which became *chocolate* in English. This seems likely, since Hernando Cortés, one of the early Spanish explorers, recognized the commercial possibilities of the Mesoamerican drink as early as 1519. After tasting the drink, Cortés created a cacao plantation in Mexico. When he went back to Spain in 1528, he took cacao beans as a gift to the king of Spain. Cortés was the first to appreciate what chocolate might taste like if combined with cane sugar and other spices appetizing to the European palate. His drink was an instant sensation in the royal court. Within a century, royalty and nobility throughout Europe enjoyed the adaptation to an ancient drink of the Maya: chocolate!

approaches. The technique also serves to enrich the soil, at least for a season or two. Thus, using the ancient techniques and tools in the same region demonstrates how the early Maya had the time to develop complex mathematics and calendars, as well as construct massive stone structures without traditional tools or transportation devices. In short, maize allowed the Maya to be who they were and to achieve all they accomplished.

MAYA TRADE

Within Maya society was a privileged class, those who engaged in trading. These merchants, called *ppolms*, traded over land and sea. The Maya lived in the right place at the right time to take advantage of the key factor in business: location. Situated directly in the corridor between the markets of the large Mexican cities and the raw materials of Central America were the Maya. The Maya took part in long-distance trade with other cultures within Mesoamerica, from as far south as present-day Colombia to as far north as central Mexico on land and islands in the Caribbean on sea. Likewise, Maya traders also conducted business between other Maya cities.

Southern Maya apparently inherited an ongoing trade network when they settled in the lowlands along the Pacific coast in the middle to late Preclassic Period. Merchants traded within a network from and through Maya lands as early as 300 B.C. This trade network followed a linear route that connected El Salvador with Mexico. The main route paralleled the Boca Costa region in Guatemala. As the Maya developed, they expanded their trade to other Maya city-states in the highlands. These connections grew and were firmly in place at the beginning of the Classic Period. Over time, traders altered their routes, depending upon warfare and alliances.

Maya traders enjoyed the fruits of the land, which supplied products as varied as the land in which the Maya lived. From the Maya highlands came jade, obsidian, quetzal feathers, and pyrite. The southern Maya coastal regions produced cacao, coral, shells, and stingray spines (which were used for bloodletting rites). From the coasts of Yucatán came salt. The currency of choice was cacao beans, which grew throughout Maya lands.

Land traders followed the established and familiar trails connecting the Maya city-states with each other and other cultures in the region. The sea traders used large fleets of canoes to transport their goods. The strength of Maya trade probably kept the expanding Aztec empire at bay.

Since the Aztec limited their military conquest once they reached the edge of Maya territory, it seems likely that the trading relationships helped preserve Maya independence in the face of Aztec power and expansion.

The Maya were in an advantageous position for trade, as they could conduct business with people in Mexico, South America, and the Caribbean. Maya traders frequently made offerings of jade, feathers, and coral to ensure a steady flow of goods and business.

Maya traders continued to supply the Aztec with cacao beans, copper tools, plumes of the quetzal bird (highly regarded by the Aztec in their religious ceremonies), and salt. These products enriched the Aztec empire. Since the Aztec did not have to develop and produce these items, it may have been easier for them to allow the Maya to retain their independence from Aztec control, as long as the products continued to flow along the trade routes.

Maya merchants did not sign written contracts sealing their deals. Instead, they made verbal agreements, sealed in public with a drinking ceremony—similar to making a toast. These verbal pacts carried with them the force of law. Since trading agreements included prominent individuals or families from two or more city-states, breaking such an agreement served as cause for war.

Maya beliefs included Ek Chuah, the patron god of merchants. Depictions of Ek Chuah show him as a black-painted god carrying a pack filled with merchandise. He is also the god of cacao beans, which were so valuable that Maya traders used them as currency. Ek Chuah oversaw the deals and contracts of land traders. Since contracts were tied to Maya religious beliefs, it was the sacred responsibility of each trader to behave with integrity. However, then as now, the temptation of valuable cargo was a compelling one. Again, the prospect of war loomed as a consequence for failing to meet contractual obligations for merchant traders.

Cities of the Classic Period

During the Classic Period, A.D. 250 to 900, within the lowland jungles of Central America, there arose strong Maya city-states. These urban centers featured large pyramids, temples, ball courts, and palaces. In addition, the Maya developed an intricate written language carved in stone pillars, called stelae. These stone records include important events in Maya history and celebrate the achievements of rulers. The stelae also serve as a window into ancient Maya culture of the Classic Period.

Three Maya cities of the Classic Period symbolize the power achievements of the Maya civilization. Tikal, Copán, and Palenque are each examples of the architectural advancements of the pre-Columbian Maya. Today, pyramids, palaces, ball courts, and other stone structures still stand in these locations. Each site also contains stelae detailing the rise of these communities. Now the cities are nothing more than ruins, but the remains remind modern researchers of the accomplishments and successes of the ancient Maya more than 1,000 years ago. The three cities of Tikal, Copán, and Palenque are all examples of Maya art, architecture, and engineering capabilities of the Classic Period. These three cities also have unique characteristics that give insight into the civilization that no longer exists.

TIKAL

The largest of the Maya cities during the Classic Period was Tikal. The city served as the primary center for ceremonies and rituals. Tikal was located in what is now northern Guatemala. Tikal was the center of one of the most powerful Maya kingdoms. Today, the Tikal National Park encompasses a vast region, more than 222 square miles (575 sq. km), including the ruins of the ancient city.

The city was founded during the Preclassic Period, as early as the fourth century B.C., but grew to become a large and influential center by the end of the third century A.D. There is evidence that Teotihuacán, the great city-state to the north, briefly conquered Tikal in the fourth century. However, the city made a comeback, expelling the Teotihuacán conquerors and reasserting its independence and power in the region. At its height in A.D. 700, Tikal served as the seat of power over the nearby chiefdoms, growing to a population of more than 60,000 people, perhaps as large as 90,000. The city was the center of political power, military might, and economic commerce throughout the Maya region. Also, Tikal conducted trade throughout Mesoamerica, including with Teotihuacán.

CHICHÉN ITZÁ

The giant temple pyramid of Chichén Itzá is one of the most remarkable structures of its kind in the world. The pyramid is the most dominant feature of the ruins at the Chichén Itzá site. The Spanish called the pyramid El Castillo, but it is also known as the Temple of Kukulkán. The structure is actually made up of two structures, one built over the other. The outer pyramid was built over an older, earlier temple. The Temple of Kukulkán is a great example of Maya integration of the calendar into their architecture. The pyramid is approximately 180 feet (55 m) tall. Each side has steps—at one time, each of the four sides had 91 steps. The combined number of steps from all four sides, along with the top platform equals 365, the number of days in the solar year. Additionally, the temple complex includes 18 terraces, symbolizing the 18 months of the Maya religious calendar, the *tzolkin*. The pyramid also boasts 52 panels, likely representing the 52 years of the Maya calendar cycle. Another extraordinary feature of this pyramid is its specific orientation, which allowed the Maya to observe the spring and autumn equinoxes.

Tikal was the largest of the Maya cities and served as the civilization's center for ceremonies and rituals. Located in modern-day Guatemala, the ruins of this city are the largest urban remnants of the Maya and feature the Temple of the Jaguar.

The rulers of Tikal channeled their resources into massive construction projects to memorialize their ancestors, building large temples containing tombs, in much the same way as the ancient Egyptians and their colossal pyramids. Construction in Tikal continued until two other states, Calakmul and Caracol, challenged Tikal's position. The ensuing conflict temporarily interrupted Tikal's construction, until the rise of the ruler Hasaw Kan K'awiil (sometimes spelled Jasaw Chan K'awiil I) in A.D. 682. Hasaw Kan K'awiil defeated a rival city-state, Calakmul, in 695. Under his leadership, Tikal again entered a period of construction and enjoyed prosperity. This resurgence enabled Tikal to endure for nearly two more centuries.

Tikal was abandoned during what many scholars call the Maya collapse, a period in which many cities were deserted and Maya culture declined. The Maya collapse occurred sometime during the latter part of the 800s. The decline of Tikal ended the city's political dominance of the Maya in central Petén. There were no more major construction projects by the close of the Classic Period. The city's population began a gradual decline, and archaeologists have uncovered evidence that at least some of the palace complexes were burned during this time. The Maya abandoned Tikal in the late tenth century.

Tikal remains the key Maya site for modern archaeologists, in large part because the city was occupied for several centuries and served as such a central point for many rituals and traditions. Stelae also record a long, continuous line of Maya rulers, which has helped explain many of the discovered tombs at the site. The vast size of the site continues to provide opportunities for archaeologists to uncover aspects of Maya culture.

Tikal covered an area of about 6.2 square miles (16 sq. km) and featured some 3,000 buildings. Situated along an east-west trade route that traveled across the Yucatán Peninsula, the city reaped the benefits of its location. The city was located in the swampy lowlands amidst a series of parallel limestone ridges, and early inhabitants constructed their largest and most important buildings on higher ground. Raised roads elevated above the swampy lowland link many of the ancient buildings. Other possible reasons for the location of the city include the fertile soil, which allowed the local inhabitants to rely on agriculture. There are also large numbers of kapok trees, which the Maya viewed as sacred, in the area.

One of the most amazing features of the city was its limited water resources. In the surrounding area, there are no lakes, rivers, or springs to supply water. Other than rainfall collection stored in 10 large reservoirs, the city had no water supply. Technological innovation allowed the ancient Maya to build one of the largest urban centers in the world at the time, in an area that was forced to rely upon storing seasonal rainfall to supply all of its water needs. This dependence upon rainfall posed risks to Tikal during periods of extended drought. Such a drought might have been a cause for the eventual demise of the city. During the twentieth century, archaeologists turned to the ancient Maya to solve their own water problems. Amazingly, archaeologists restored one of the 10 reservoirs and used it for their own needs, tapping into Tikal's average rainfall of more than 76 inches (193 cm).

A valuable resource found in Tikal was flint. Flint is a hard, rocklike mineral that the Maya used to fashion weapons and tools. Flint is hard enough that tools made from it would be useful for stone cutting. Such a material was necessary for the ancient Maya to build the large stone buildings they constructed throughout the Classic Period.

COPÁN

The second-greatest Maya city of the Classic Period was Copán, located in present-day western Honduras, near Guatemala. Copán was the capital city for the southernmost kingdom, situated in the far southeast region

JAGUAR: SYMBOL OF THE NIGHT

The Maya living within the jungles of Mesoamerica during the Classic Period were familiar with the jaguar. These large jungle cats are the only of the *Panthera* species native to the Americas. These members of the feline family are large and fierce. Only the tiger and lion are larger. Today, jaguars are found from northern Argentina to northern Mexico, possibly even into the state of Arizona. Then and now, local inhabitants sharing the territory with jaguars respect the size and capabilities of these ferocious predators.

The ancient Maya adopted the jaguar as a symbol of political strength and power in warfare. They also included the jaguar in their religious beliefs, giving it a prominent place within their mythology stories. That the Maya did this should not be surprising. Jaguars are often found near water, as they are one of the few large cats that enjoy swimming and hunting in the water. Since the Maya lived in areas that lacked consistent rainfall, they often observed jaguars in the wild and in the water.

The jaguar possesses an extremely powerful bite, even more so than other large felines. This characteristic allows the jaguar to pierce the shells of armored reptiles, something no other big cat can accomplish. Lions and other big cats often bite the neck of their prey to make the kill. In contrast, the jaguar has such a strong bite that it will usually bite its prey on the head, piercing the skull and killing the quarry. This mighty killer was capable of bringing down the largest prey in the Mesoamerican jungles.

containing the Mesoamerican cultures. Maya living in and around the city often found themselves surrounded by non-Maya cultures. Scholars believe the ancient Maya called the city Oxwitik, though Copán is the name most often associated with this place today. Its location allowed its residents to trade with the tribes in modern-day Panama. Archaeologists have discovered artwork, weapons, and tools made of gold and lead by Panamanian artisans from this period. Copán enjoyed its greatest years from the fifth to ninth centuries A.D., though it was continuously

Mesoamerican depictions of jaguars first appeared during the mid–Preclassic Period, as early as 1000 B.C. Early Maya admired the quick speed and agility of the fierce beast. Sporting a spotted coat of fur similar to that of a leopard, the jaguar lived as king of the Mesoamerican jungle. Many Maya representations of the jaguar highlight the Maya belief in the connection of the animal with the underworld. Since the jaguar hunted both at night and during the day, it represented the ability to move between underworld and the Earth. Many Maya gods exhibit jaguar-like characteristics, specifically to communicate their association with the underworld. As author E.P. Benson writes in *Icons of Power: Feline Symbolism in the Americas* (edited by Nicholas J. Saunders), "Maya gods with jaguar attributes or garments are underworld gods." The god Xblanque, one of the Maya hero twins, is an example. His body is covered with bits and pieces of jaguar fur.

Due to the respect given to jaguars, only the ruling class was allowed to wear its fur. Indeed, jaguar pelts came to symbolize royalty. Some rulers adopted the feline into their family name, such as Jaguar Paw of Tikal in the A.D. 300s. The only others within Maya society allowed to wear jaguar pelts were mighty hunters and warriors. These men were held in high esteem and also adorned themselves with teeth and claws from the revered symbol of the Maya, the jaguar.

inhabited for over 2,000 years, from the early Preclassic to the Postclassic periods.

The ruins at Copán boast an architectural style that includes some of the finest examples of Maya art and sculptures, including colored murals, vases, and a variety of carved-stone decorations, all made by skilled artisans. Natural erosion from the Copán River has claimed much of the eastern section of the city. In the 1930s, engineers diverted the river in an effort to protect the remaining objects and buildings at the site.

In A.D. 738, the city experienced a major upheaval when a rival king from Quiriguá captured, then put to death, one of Copán's great kings, Uaxaclajuun Ub'aah K'awiil. This setback led to about 17 years of turmoil and subjugation at the hands of Quiriguá. However, following this disruption, the city once again undertook large construction projects. Once major construction ended, the city remained occupied, but the population suffered a steady decline throughout the eighth and ninth centuries until only about 5,000 people remained in the city. By the time the Spanish arrived and made contact with locals in the sixteenth century, Copán was deserted, with only a few small villages in the area.

Copán lies among foothills within a fertile valley. During the Preclassic Period, the Copán Valley was swampy, unlevel, and subject to seasonal flooding. In the Early Classic Period, its people took steps to protect the buildings from flooding and make the valley floor level. These renovations included five esplanades, or wide walkways, that served as large plazas, or open areas, within the city.

During the Late Classic Period, the city of Copán covered an area of about 0.23 square miles (0.6 sq. km) and boasted a population of at least 20,000 people. The outlying residences stretched 9 square miles (23.4 sq. km). In contrast, the city of Tikal alone was two-thirds the size of the outlying area of Copán. Tikal covered more than 6 square miles (16 sq. km).

The layout of Copán included 16 neighborhoods stemming from the center of the city, like spokes on a wheel. At the center is the acropolis, or central courtyard, the most stunning feature of Copán uncovered at the site. The main courtyard included a network of palaces, temples, pyramids, and plazas. Surrounding this city center were stone seats, arranged in tiers, allowing thousands to gather and observe ceremonies in Copán. Also found at the site are many altars and stelae, which include

The 63 exterior steps on the central temple of Copán, the second-largest Maya city, are known as the Hieroglyphic Stairway. Intricately carved with Maya imagery, many scholars believe that the Maya calendar was developed here.

hieroglyphic writings commemorating rulers and their accomplishments. A large ball court has also been uncovered within the acropolis.

One of the most important finds in the acropolis is the Hieroglyphic Stairway, containing 63 steps. Carved hieroglyphics cover each stone step. Located on every tenth step was a stone statue portraying a Maya god, ruler, or some other notable person. Copán was also the scientific center for the ancient Maya. Scholars believe that it was there that the famous Maya calendar was developed.

Early Maya were interested in astronomy, the study of the heavens. The sundial was an important tool in astronomy for these ancient people. A sundial is a mechanism that calculates time by the position of the sun in the sky. Throughout the day, as the sun moves throughout the sky, the shadow cast on the sundial markings indicates the time of day. This kind of artifact has been discovered in Copán.

PALENQUE

The third and last great Maya city-state that will be examined is Palenque. At times described as a highland site, Palenque lies just 1,000 feet (305 m) above sea level. The site is in a tropical rain forest within the modern-day state of Chiapas, Mexico. Palenque is distinctive from Copán in that there are very few stelae there. However, the site does include an impressive structure, the Temple of Inscriptions. The temple is a magnificent tomb for K'inich Janaab' Pakal, a great ruler of the city. K'inich (which means "Sun-faced") Janaab' Pakal ascended to power at the age of 12 in A.D. 615.

The tomb within the Temple of Inscriptions was discovered in the 1940s during a restoration project of the inner chamber of the temple. Alberto Ruz Lhuillier, a Mexican archaeologist, detected holes in the temple floor. These holes, once cleared of stone plugs, allowed the stone slab to be lifted up. Upon lifting the slab, Lhuillier found a shaft filled with rocks, stone, and dirt. Lhuillier and his team worked four digging seasons to remove the debris, eventually revealing a stairway. Lhuillier uncovered the last of the staircase in 1952. There, he and his team found the skeletons of five or six young adults in a short hallway. Researchers believe the skeletons are the remains of human sacrifices. At the end of the corridor was a large, triangle-shaped stone slab serving as a door to a chamber beyond. Behind this stone slab was the tomb of Pakal the Great.

The tomb of K'inich Janaab' Pakal, a Maya ruler, can be found in the civilization's third-largest city, Palenque. Discovered in 1952, the tomb of Pakal is inside the Tomb of Inscriptions, where archaeologists discovered the king's remains covered with jewelry, precious stones, and a jade face mask fashioned to look like him.

Historian Gavin Menzies recounts what Lhuillier later wrote of the day he entered the tomb:

Out of the dim shadows emerged a vision from a fairytale, a fantastic ethereal sight from another world. It seemed a huge magic grotto, carved out of ice, the walls sparkling and glistening like snow crystals . . . the impression, in fact, was that of an abandoned chapel. Across the walls marched stucco figures in low relief. Then my eyes sought the floor. This was almost entirely filled with the great carved stone slab in perfect condition. . . . Ours were the first eyes that had gazed on it in more than a thousand years!

The chamber was about 30 feet (9 m) long, 13 feet wide (4 m), and 23 feet (7 m) high. Within this room, the large, carved stone slab was indeed an impressive sight. However, there was more to the large stone slab floor than initially appeared. The carved slab was the lid to a sarcophagus, or coffin, made of limestone. Inside the sarcophagus were the decorated remains of Pakal the Great.

The remains were decorated with jewelry such as rings and bracelets, a breastplate, and even earplugs made of jade. The skeleton also displayed signs typical of Maya nobility, including the bright red teeth and bones, accomplished by cinnabar, a red mercury ore. The most impressive artwork adorning the dead king's remains was the face mask, fashioned to look like Pakal. Made of jade with small pieces of obsidian and shell for the eyes, the mask is an exceptional piece of Maya artisanship.

In 684, Pakal's son, K'inich Kan B'alam ascended the throne at age 48. Kan B'alam completed the work on his father's tomb during his 18-year reign. However, soon after, during the eighth century, Palenque increasingly found itself clashing with Toniná, a rival kingdom located 45 miles (64 km) south. This ongoing conflict weakened the city, perhaps contributing to its decline. The last known ruler of Palenque was Janaab' Pakal III, who took the throne in 799. At this time, researchers know little about his reign or how the city collapsed.

The Collapse

Although the Maya civilization encompassed a large area, there was no empire of the Maya. Instead, throughout the Classic Period, about 250 B.C. until A.D. 900, Maya territory was simply a group of city-states that found themselves in almost constant warfare with each other. Throughout this period, no one state managed to establish itself as the dominant city over all the other Maya city-states. Occasionally, a city-state enjoyed dominance over nearby city-states, but the continual fighting only weakened each contestant. As a result, even the stronger city-states found themselves too weak to assert and maintain control over other city-states for very long. Much like the ancient Greeks, Maya city-states shared a common language, religious beliefs, and many cultural traits, but each was separate and independent from the others. Further, each city-state appeared bent on gaining dominance over other city-states on the field of battle.

The apparent need to dominate another city-state stems from Maya religious beliefs and cultural views of honor. Maya society respected rulers who defeated enemies on the field of battle. Even the ceremonial execution of a captured ruler was done to honor the captive by spilling his blood. According to Maya beliefs, a noble warrior deserved to die.

Despite the fighting for domination among city-states, boundaries changed little after decades of fighting. This was primarily due to the desire to win the battle in order to capture prisoners, not to extend an empire. Thus, warfare was not about gaining land or capturing a city. Warfare of the Maya Classic Period instead centered on capturing enemy warriors, especially the king. Once a king fell into the hands of his enemy, the battle was over. A captured king faced torture and death. Once captured by his rivals, a ruler knew the fate that awaited him: public torture followed by death either from beheading or on the sacrificial altar of his enemies. Nevertheless, the result was his death at the hands of his foes, who celebrated their victory at his expense.

Sometimes, Maya city-states made alliances and truces with other city-states. These alliances were usually sealed through marriage between members of the ruling family. Scholars know of several notable marriage alliances between Maya city-states. Perhaps the most significant was the marriage of a bride from Tikal who was given in marriage to the ruling family in Naranjo. Scroll Squirrel was a son from that marriage. Scroll Squirrel later married a woman from the ruling class in Tikal, further strengthening the bond between the two city-states.

MAYA WARRIORS AND WARFARE

Entering into battle, Maya warriors wore brightly colored parrot feathers atop a wooden helmet. The higher a warrior's status in Maya society, the more brightly he decorated himself for battle. His armor was made of quilted cotton, soaked in salt water to increase its durability and strength against enemy weapons. The Spanish were so impressed by the effectiveness of the Maya armor that they shed their heavy metal armor and adopted the lighter-weight cotton armor of the natives.

The typical Maya warrior was armed with a war club made of wood. His club usually included one or more blades, made of obsidian. Each warrior also carried a sling and stones to attack from a distance. Also part of his long-range arsenal was a spear-thrower to launch deadly darts from farther away. For hand-to-hand fighting, the Maya warrior carried knives, usually one with a flint blade, as well as a shell knife with three distinct blades.

Success in Maya warfare rested on the element of surprise. Maya city-states did not declare war on their enemies or announce that they intended to fight. Instead, their armies advanced into enemy territory as secretly as possible. This tactic allowed them to seize prisoners and valuables, which was the primary goal of warfare. The city-state's ruler, his closest fighting men, priests, and other warriors of higher social class led the battle from the center of the advancing line. Warriors from lower classes rounded out the ranks on either side.

Fierce and resourceful, Maya warriors used natural resources to protect and arm themselves in battle. They wore durable, light cotton robes for armor and used strong weapons to attack their enemies. Any other decorations, such as brightly colored feathers, designated their social class.

Once the battle began, it was a noisy affair. The struggle was violent and ferocious as soldiers struggled to gain an advantage and capture prisoners. Some blew conch shells and whistles, while others beat drums. Men cried out as they struggled in battle. Maya battles were indeed loud events.

THE MAYA FIGHTING SEASON

All Maya, regardless of which city-state they were allegiant to, relied upon agriculture as their primary food source. As a result, conflict with other city-states occurred outside the planting and harvesting seasons. The Maya fighting season usually took place after planting and before the harvest. If a campaign took too long, a leader faced the prospect of his farmer-warriors abandoning him in order to tend to the fields back home. For most Maya warriors, campaigns were short, with enemies no more than a day's march away. Warfare did not occur every day, but it was a regular and annual part of Maya life.

COLLAPSE

One of the greatest archaeological mysteries is the cause of the Classic Maya collapse. The Maya of the Classic Period enjoyed a rich cultural heritage with advanced technology and scientific knowledge. Scholars refer to the Classic Maya collapse as the last 100 years of the Classic Period, or A.D. 800 to 900. During this century, Maya cities in the southern lowlands steadily declined. By or shortly after A.D. 900, residents abandoned most of these cities. The most visible indication of decline was the end of major public works projects, such as causeways, pyramids, palaces, and ball courts. The construction of monuments and their inscriptions, invaluable to archaeologists, also ended.

While the southern cities of the Maya collapsed, others in the northern highlands continued to endure. Indeed, several Maya cities persisted for several centuries. Chichén Itzá united the northern Yucatán region, bringing peace and prosperity for a time. The Classic Maya civilization lasted until the Spanish finally conquered the last independent city-state, Tayasal, in 1697. Due to the continuance of the Maya culture in the north and in some outlying areas, some scholars reject the idea of a collapse. Historian E.W. Andrews IV states his belief that "no such thing happened."

There are dozens of theories and variations of theories that attempt to explain the Classic Maya collapse. None of these explanations has been universally accepted. The theories generally fall into the following areas: outside invaders, unrest from within, or a failed economy. More specifically, the theories include these ideas: an outside group invaded the Maya, the Maya fell due to internal pressures and unrest, there was a breakdown in the Maya trade routes that resulted in a failed economy, disease decimated the population centers, prolonged drought weakened the agricultural economy, or a widespread ecological disaster resulted in the collapse.

In some places of the Yucatán, there is archaeological evidence that the Toltec, a group that served as the foundation for another later power, the Aztec, entered the region by force, which may help explain the Maya collapse. A variation of this theory is the idea that a group of foreign invaders entered and established control over the Maya in the southern lowlands. This non-Maya group of invaders were not the Toltec but resembled them in several ways. This Toltec or Toltec-like group appears to have attacked and invaded parts of the Maya region beginning in the early ninth century, but there had been considerable interaction between the two groups well before that time. Thus, it is not likely that an armed conflict between the two led to the demise of the Classic Maya, at least not in every city-state. In addition, most scholars reject the suggestion that invasion by foreigners led to the collapse, since the decline occurred gradually over the course of several decades. Usually, the fall of a civilization from invasion takes place rapidly as the foreign force overruns and overwhelms the defenders.

Another set of theories asserts that the Maya fell from internal unrest. This approach does not explain what became of the population. There is evidence suggesting that the number of Maya in the region decreased. Some scholars question this aspect, claiming the population should have increased with the lessening of obligations to the ruling class. Since most revolts lead to a change in leadership, it is curious that no new leadership emerged during the collapse. In addition, if there was unrest that led to the fall of the traditional power structure, the surviving stone records do not include any details of such events.

Others, such as Michel Peissel, believe that the city-state of Chichén Itzá established dominance over the Yucatán, which led to the collapse. According to this theory, the rise of Chichén Itzá resulted in a shift in the trading routes of cacao, from overland to coastal sea routes. This alteration destroyed the economy of the inland cities, leading to their decline and abandonment. This theory might explain why the Maya did

BALL COURTS

Ball courts are perhaps the most common architectural feature in Maya cities. Archaeologists have found ball courts in virtually every Maya settlement, large or small. It appears that the ancient Maya played and observed the playing of a ball game that held religious and ceremonial meaning to them. Ball courts that have been excavated come in various sizes, though most are a rectangular shape. Seven ball courts have been discovered in Chichén Itzá, six of which were still in use at the end of that city's independence from Spanish rule. Each court is sized differently, with the smallest being 65 feet long and 20 feet wide (about 20 m by 6 m). The largest court in Chichén Itzá had a playing field of 480 feet by 120 feet (146 m by 36 m), with the structure itself even larger.

Ball courts consisted of walls made of stone, usually sloped toward the playing field. In the center of each of the long side walls was a stone ring, set at a 90 degree angle to the ground. The ring's opening faced each end of the field or the opposing teams. The object of the game was to send the ball through the stone ring. The ball was made of rubber. When the Spanish first observed these balls, it was the first time Europeans had seen rubber. Rules for the game apparently prohibited touching the ball with the hands

not universally collapse, but instead only certain city-states deteriorated. Since some Maya cities prospered during the collapse of others and many of these thriving cities were located on the coastal sea routes used by Chichén Itzá traders, the theory seems plausible.

To demonstrate the possibility of the Maya switching to coastal trade, in 1988 a team of researchers traveled 404 miles (650 km) in a Maya dugout from Chunyaxché in Quintana Roo, Mexico, to Belize to the Mojo River. Did a group of Maya simply shift the way in which goods were transported through the region? If so, did this change in the mode of transportation result in the abandonment of entire cities? Researchers may never know.

or feet. Instead, players had to hit the ball with the hip, wrist, or elbow. Contestants wore leather padding to protect their bodies from the pounding of the hard rubber ball. The game was extremely difficult. According to the earliest rules, a player fortunate enough to score a point received the clothing and jewelry of every spectator. It appears that a team won by scoring points or committing fewer infractions, since the stated objective of getting the ball through the ring was virtually impossible on some of the larger ball courts.

Ball courts appear throughout Maya ruins, indicating the game was played throughout the region. However, the game was far more serious than most games. The losing team met their end as human sacrifices! Some scholars believe it was the leader of the winning team that was sacrificed. Researchers are unsure, since what is now known of the game comes through pictures and carvings depicting the events. It is possible that the courts merely served as a location for religious rituals, including sacrifices. Some Maya mythological stories describe a game in which two twin brothers, playing the part of the heroes, deceive and defeat the gods of the underworld in a game very similar to the ball game.

Other scholars point to the possibility that disease led to the downfall of the Maya. An epidemic would explain the population losses. However, there are no records indicating that disease was an ongoing concern or problem to the Maya. Scholars speculate that some parasite or germ-carrying insects infected the Maya. Most scholars who think disease contributed to the Maya collapse believe it was a contributing factor to the weakening of the civilization, not the primary reason for the decline.

The drought theories are relatively simple. Since the Maya relied heavily on agriculture for their sustenance, a prolonged drought would certainly explain the collapse. Archaeological digs have confirmed that the Maya built reservoirs, aqueducts, and other kinds of structures necessary for holding water. More recent archaeological evidence demonstrates the Maya also used irrigation techniques such as canals. Many of the ruins are located near sinkholes holding water. The evidence points to the Maya knowing the importance of water to their economy. An extended period with little or no rain makes sense. However, like each of the groups of theories, there is no record written in stone supporting it.

The last group of theories includes the idea that some sort of ecological disaster led to the collapse. Specifically, the land simply could not support the level of population. Under this theory, the slash-and-burn techniques eventually depleted the soil. Other evidences include deforestation and loss of diversity in plant and animal life. However, the Maya had sustained themselves with these methods for hundreds of years, so the sudden decline in less than a century likely required some other condition.

So what was the cause of the decline of the Maya civilization? Experts continue to dispute the cause. In part, this disagreement stems from the approach that there is one reason for the Maya collapse. It appears that many scholars hope to explain the fall of each of the Maya city-states. The difficulty in this approach is that the Maya did not have a single unified central power that controlled all Maya territory. Instead, the civilization comprised individual city-states that enjoyed local self-rule. Further complicating things for historians, these individual city-states shared most, if not all, of the primary traits of culture that researchers use to understand a civilization. Thus, present-day scholars are studying a collection of city-states attempting to explain the decline of all the city-states. Thus far, this has proved to be an impossible task.

It seems more likely that each city-state weakened and deteriorated for various reasons. In some cases, neighboring city-states waned for the same reason or reasons. In other cases, city-states might have slowly died for reasons very different from those of nearby city-states. When one considers that most researchers and the archaeological evidence have all but eliminated the possibility of a hostile takeover, then the idea that an assortment of problems contributed to the Maya collapse seems all the more likely.

The answer to the actual cause of the Maya collapse might never be known. However, it is known that virtually all of the city-states fell due to one of several reasons: shifts in trade routes, deforestation, overpopulation of a local area, weakened states due to nearly constant warring, and extended periods of drought, to name a few. The few city-states that survived then faced the threat of European dominance when the Spanish arrived and began their conquest in the 1520s.

THE SPANISH CONQUEST

When Spanish explorers first arrived on the Mexican mainland in the 1510s, they found the Aztec with an established system of government led by their leader, Montezuma. The Spaniards also found a crumbling empire. Aztec religious beliefs and practices contributed to the weakened state of the empire. These religious practices demanded human sacrifices, and warfare produced captives for these sacrificial rituals. The result was that the Aztec empire found itself in an almost constant state of intertribal warfare. With no outside threats, the Aztec leadership managed to balance and manipulate these tribal tensions in order to maintain control. The arrival of the Spanish upset that balance. Now another power offered an alternative to tribes seeking to rid themselves of Aztec domination. The presence of the powerful Spanish, complete with firearms and horses, presented an opportunity to end Aztec rule over the various tribes.

The allure of freedom from Aztec rule was too much for most tribes to resist. What these tribes did not understand is that the Spanish did not intend to free the tribes, but rather to replace the Aztec as the power controlling the empire. And like the Aztec, the Spanish used religion to impose and maintain their power over the peoples of Mesoamerica.

Unlike the Aztec, the Maya did not have a centralized government to unify around to ward off Spanish attempts to establish control of the region. However, the lack of an identifiable leadership made it difficult for the Spaniards to defeat and control the Maya. In contrast, the Aztec had an identifiable ruler in Montezuma. Once he defeated Montezuma, Hernando Cortés simply replaced the Aztec sovereign as the ruler of the empire. Various Spanish explorers arrived in Maya territory hoping to establish control over the region. Instead, these would-be conquerors found that even if they defeated a Maya force, there was no easy way to establish rule over the Maya.

The first contact between the Spanish and Maya took place in 1502 during the fourth and final journey of Christopher Columbus to the New World. Columbus's son was with a party of Spaniards who encountered a Maya trading canoe off the coast of what is now Honduras. The canoe was constructed from a single large tree trunk. When the Spaniards approached the canoe, there were more than two dozen people in it, along with goods for trading. The Europeans seized the canoe in order to examine the goods and found copper items, obsidian blades, cloth garments, pottery, flint tools, and cacao beans. The Maya did all they could to keep the cacao beans from falling into Spanish hands. The Spanish released the Maya and their canoe, but it was not long before the Europeans began to wonder about possible treasures in the land of the Maya.

Francisco Hernández de Córdoba was the first Spaniard to explore the regions of the Maya. In 1517, Córdoba left Cuba, the seat of Spanish presence in the New World, in hopes of finding a source of natives to replace the many slaves who had died from disease. After seeing stone cities on the coastline of Yucatán, Córdoba landed and made contact with many of the natives. These encounters went well until the Maya ambushed Córdoba and about 80 of his men at Cape Cotoche. Córdoba and his group, many of them injured, returned to Cuba with tales of possible treasures, though they had acquired only a few gold trinkets.

The governor of Cuba sent another expedition of about 240 men, led by Juan de Grijalva. Like the Córdoba expedition, this one managed to land and make contact with the natives in several places, but ultimately Grijalva found nothing noteworthy. He returned to Cuba empty-handed, but brought tales of great riches farther inland. There was no basis for these tales, other than the hope that there might be gold and other treasures awaiting them farther west. His reports spurred Hernando Cortés to lead an expedition against the Aztec in 1519.

In 1527, Francisco de Montejo, a veteran of both the Grijalva and Cortés expeditions, landed in eastern Yucatán and attempted to impose Spanish rule there. However, Montejo found it difficult to engage and defeat the Maya. After raising more than one force and struggling for several years, Montejo finally abandoned his efforts in 1535. However, five years later his son, Francisco de Montejo the Younger, took up the cause. The younger Montejo raised a large army and invaded the Yucatán. In 1542, he seized the Maya city of Tho, renaming it Mérida and making it his capital. Montejo managed to make allies with some of the Maya leaders in western Yucatán, converting them to Roman Catholicism. All went well for a time, but the weight of Spanish rule soon led to revolt. Officially, the revolt was put down in 1546, but resistance continued for another 150 years. The

The arrival of Spanish conquistadors in the New World was the first exposure the Maya had to Europeans and firearms. The Spaniards quickly conquered the Maya, but the Spanish rulers violently stamped out slave revolts, which continued to spring up for decades.

Maya continued to rebel, until the last major uprising was defeated in 1697 when the Spanish and their Indian allies captured the city of Tayasal, the last independent Maya city.

Religious Beliefs
and Practices

The Maya held religious beliefs that permeated almost every aspect of their lives. Much like some of the later Mesoamerican cultures, such as the Aztec and Inca, the Maya assumed that all things happened according to a divine will and occurred, and sometimes reoccurred, in a cycle. Religious customs were directly connected to the astronomical cycles the Maya observed in the sky. The Maya went so far as to keep a separate calendar that recorded and predicted these natural cycles. Priests enjoyed high social status because they could interpret and predict the times as either good or bad, based upon their calendars. Since the common people lacked the ability to figure out the meanings of the calendars, priests held influence over them. In addition, the ruling class looked to priests to determine the timing of important ceremonies and other undertakings.

THE GROWTH OF MAYA GODS

In the early years, prior to the Classic Period, Maya religious beliefs simply embodied nature and the elements within the nomadic lifestyle in which the people lived. These religious practices needed only casual and unceremonious forms and structures. Under these circumstances, there was no need for an organized priesthood or sophisticated rites, nor did these early Maya need temples, shrines, or other places of worship. Instead of a formal priesthood, each head of each family served as the priest for that family. Temporary homes for residents meant temporary places of worship. According the historian Sylvanus Griswold Morley, the Lacandon Maya, who live in the forests of the Usumacinta Valley in eastern Chiapas, still practice religious rites in this way.

However, as the Maya shifted into a settled, agriculturally based lifestyle, religious beliefs became more complex. A formal priesthood replaced the informal family heads as spiritual leaders within the community. The settled lifestyle and economy allowed religion to become more formal. Indeed, the agriculturally based lifestyle virtually demanded that religion become more formal and complex. People now lived in one place, and the desire for more prestigious and grand places of worship grew. A trained and qualified group of priests was now needed to care for the temples and to understand and explain the desires of the gods to the common people. Accompanying the rise of a professional priesthood were ceremonies that were more lavish and greater demands on the people to support their religion. Over time, the Maya advanced concepts and ideas of gods that became more and more specific and specialized. Part of this advancement included the development of a calendar, based on the patterns of the sun, the moon, and Venus. About the same time, the Maya invented their unique form of writing. All of the elements needed to elevate the Maya religion and its priests were now in place.

The Maya, like all other ancient cultures, have stories describing how they came into existence. Historians find these stories in the Popol Vuh, or Book of Advice. The Popol Vuh was the sacred book of southern Maya who lived in the highlands of present-day Guatemala. Scholars call the people who lived there the Quiché Maya. The Popol Vuh includes stories and other descriptions of gods, festivals, and religious beliefs of the Maya.

The Maya practiced a belief in many gods, or polytheism. These gods usually represented some aspect or force of nature. The Maya believed that the world was created by the god Hunab (or Hunab Ku), the father of Itzamná. Under Maya beliefs, Hunab created the world but then existed in a faraway place and took a rather detached view of creation. Hunab supposedly used maize to form humankind, emphasizing the important link between corn and the Maya existence. Although Itzamná was the son of Hunab, he was viewed as the greatest of the Maya gods. Itzamná was associated with those things thought to improve life for humankind, such as fire, medicine, science, and writing. Itzamná is the only Maya god not linked to death or destruction. This god rejected all violence, wars, and human sacrifices. All other Maya gods represent some darker side of life.

Itzamná stands alone as a giver and provider of life, justifying his place as the supreme god in Maya religious beliefs. Itzamná ruled the sky, and other dark gods ruled the underworld.

Another god represented in the Maya stone carvings and in the few surviving writings was Chac, the god of rain and lightning. In a culture that depended so heavily upon agriculture for its survival, the need for rain elevated the stature of this god within the pantheon of deities. The Maya had gods for almost every natural occurrence and life event. The Maya even had a god of chocolate! Maya rulers served as representatives of the gods to the people and of the people to the gods. The Maya believed their rulers to be semidivine.

Maya religious beliefs included three primary places: the Earth, the heavens, and the underworld. According to Maya beliefs, the afterlife was dangerous for the soul as it journeyed through the underworld. Inhabited by evil gods, the underworld was represented in Maya carvings by the jaguar, which symbolized the night. Under Maya belief, all went to the underworld when they died. The only exceptions were those who died in childbirth or had been sacrificed, in which case they journeyed into heaven. All other souls arrived at the underworld through caves. Nighttime and anything dark was considered to symbolize or be a pathway into the underworld.

One interesting characteristic of Maya religious beliefs is that of good and evil within the deities. Gods were not always good, nor were they always evil. Instead of a stable list of rights and wrongs, actions, traits, and attitudes shifted between preferred and undesirable. Sometimes, evil was the desirable trait, which made Maya ethics challenging, even for the Maya. The calendar cycles determined which actions or course was acceptable. A satisfactory action on one date in a given cycle might be considered unacceptable in another. This is foundational to the power the priests held over their fellow countrymen.

The Maya believed that everything in history followed cycles. This meant that they believed knowing their past gave them the knowledge needed to understand the present and predict the future. The calendars they developed held the keys to understanding these cycles. Since the gods did not always act in the best interests of humans, the Maya relied upon these cycles to determine the wisdom of undertaking endeavors on particular days.

MAYA SACRIFICES

The Maya called upon their gods using methods common in other cultures, such as fasting, abstinence, and sacrifices. Fasting was required of priests, and others in the community participated on a voluntary basis. Abstaining from sexual relations was part of the purifying rituals followed by the priests as they prepared to appeal to their gods on behalf of their people. Other forms of abstinence included fasting from meat and certain spices, especially chili pepper and salt.

One of the most important components of Maya worship was the sacrifices. These offerings varied in value and scope. A sacrifice might consist of food or an inexpensive decoration to a valuable possession or even a human. The importance of the need dictated the kind of sacrifice. Whereas food or ornaments sufficed for curing an illness or dealing with some other minor misfortune, valuable possessions or human sacrifices might be needed in times of drought that threatened the health and safety of the whole community.

The Maya rarely sacrificed humans until the Postclassic Period. Since it was during this period that the Spanish first had contact with this culture, the rituals convinced many of the newcomers that the Maya were an uncivilized culture in need of enlightenment. Although not as common as in later years, the practice was carried out during the Classic Period.

The Maya performed human sacrifices in a number of different ways. However, the most commonly depicted method, and probably the oldest form of the ritual, was the removal of the victim's heart. Priests stripped the chosen individual and painted him blue, which was the sacrificial color. Then, they placed a distinctive headdress on the victim's head and led him to the sacrificial site. Sometimes, sacrifices were conducted in the temple courtyard. Often, the sacrifices took place on an altar next to an idol, sitting atop the apex of temple pyramids.

The priests performed a ritual to cleanse the stone altar of evil spirits, and then they smeared the sacrificial blue paint on the altar. Four older men, chosen for the occasion, served as *chacs* for the sacrifice. The chacs, who were also painted blue, held the victim on the stone altar, the shape of which forced his chest upward. The four chacs held the four limbs to immobilize the victim for the *nacom*. Thus, the victim found himself held down, lying faceup on an altar with hundreds or even thousands of spectators watching as another priest, the nacom, approached him to complete the sacrifice to the nearby idol. The nacom carried an ornate flint knife in his hand, which he thrust into the victim's chest on the left side. Placing his hand into the opening, the nacom then removed the heart. The

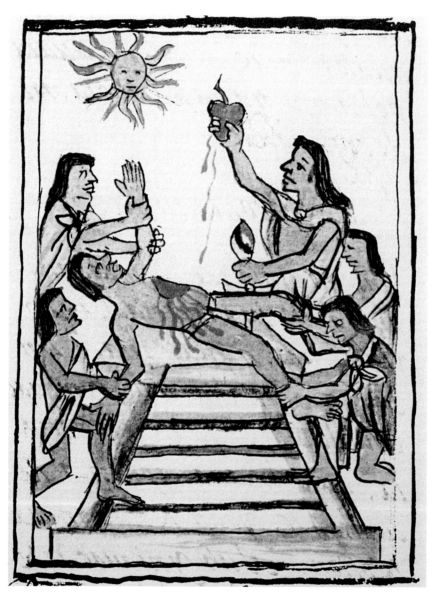

The Maya often made offerings to their gods for favorable treatment, but major events called for larger contributions. Human sacrifices were performed in a variety of ways, but the most well-known method involved removing the heart of the sacrificed victim.

nacom then handed the still-beating heart to the presiding priest, called the *chilan*, who smeared the heart's blood on the idol.

If the sacrifice occurred on top of a pyramid temple, the chacs then disposed of the body by throwing it into the courtyard below. Other priests in the courtyard then removed most of the skin from the corpse. The chilan later wore this skin as he led the spectators in a religious dance. The chilan also received the hands and feet of the victim as trophies. If the victim was a prisoner of war, some of his bones went to his captor to signify the latter's strength and bravery. Captured soldiers viewed as brave faced the same sacrifice, but as a way to honor the captured enemy soldier, members of the noble class then ate their bodies.

THE PLUMED SERPENT

The Maya believed in the feathered serpent god or the plumed serpent, called Kukulkán (called Quetzalcoatl by the Aztec). Images of this god are part of the snake shadow on the steps of El Castillo during the spring and autumn equinoxes. At the base of the pyramid, next to the steps, is a carved face of Kukulkán. The shadows that form a snakelike apparition connect behind the stone head. Given the reverence to Kukulkán in Maya beliefs, this hardly seems accidental.

MAYA DEATH RITUALS AND THE AFTERLIFE

Regardless of one's station in life, dead Maya were buried with tools and food for their journey to the afterlife. Members of the lower class were buried beneath the floors of their humble houses. Members of the nobility were wrapped in a shroud and then laid to rest in ornate tombs or large shrines, sometimes with the bodies of servants to accompany them into the afterlife. Those of the ruling class had tombs within the city center, underneath the great open courts and within some of the most impressive buildings or holy shrines. Food- and water-filled pottery containers were buried with the deceased to supply provisions for the afterlife. Usually, dried maize and jade were placed in the mouth of the corpse, giving the dead a little food and money for use in the afterlife. Once the burial spots beneath a house became filled, usually after a generation, the surviving relatives vacated the house and turned it into a shrine to honor their ancestors.

On occasion, members of the Maya nobility in the Yucatán were cremated. Wooden urns or pottery vessels held their ashes. Depictions of the deceased adorned these containers. For others, their ashes were placed within a statue of the deceased, with an empty spot in the back of the head in which the ashes or a container of ashes was placed. Cremation was usually reserved for the nobility and ruling class.

Sometimes, the Maya buried a dead man with his dog. This practice, which the Aztec later imitated, was based on the belief that the dog would provide companionship to his master on his journey through the afterlife. Mesoamerican myths also included the story of the god Quetzalcoatl (the Maya god Kukulkán), who journeyed to the underworld accompanied by his dog at his side as a guide and protector.

WATER

Many of the Maya lived in lands that received little rainfall throughout the year. There are no large rivers in the northern Yucatán Peninsula, where the dry season can last up to half a year. Beneath the surface, the land is made of limestone. Water runs through the surface and collects underground. In some locations, the surface has collapsed, leaving a sunken lake or cenote. The sinkholes attracted Maya who lived nearby. Fed by underground rivers, these cenotes provided an important source of fresh water for the early Maya.

Cenotes held a special place in Maya religious beliefs. Many believed the underground lakes to be pathways into the underworld. The most important cenote is at Chichén Itzá, which was connected with El Castillo by a stone walkway measuring 20 feet wide (6 m) and stretching some 1,000 feet (305 m) long. Consequently, Maya sometimes offered sacrifices to gods, especially the rain god Chac, by throwing the sacrifice into the sinkhole. These sacrifices included food, precious objects, and even humans. Sacrificing humans in this way was apparently an uncommon rite, but it did happen. This sacrifice occurred in response to drought, epidemic, and famine. To appease the gods, the Maya flung their live offerings into the dark cenote below. Bishop Diego de Landa wrote of this cenote, saying: "Into this well they have had, and then had, the custom of throwing men alive, as a sacrifice to the gods in times of drought, and they believed they did not die, though they never saw them again. They also threw into it many other things, like precious stones and things that they prized."

In 1901, Edward Thompson, the U.S. consul to Mérida, the capital city of the Yucatán, purchased the Chichén Itzá cenote. Thompson had

Cenotes were a major source of freshwater for the Maya, and the most sacred and important cenote is located at Chichén Itzá. The Maya would throw offerings and sacrifices to the gods into this sinkhole, hoping to improve their lives or alleviate droughts or famines.

heard stories of such sacrifices, and he dredged the cenote, finding human remains and valuable offerings made of copper, gold, and jade. Among other objects recovered were plates, cups, masks, bells, and knives. The copper and gold objects originated from places as far away as the Valley of Mexico and Colombia, offering further evidence of the widespread trading might of the Maya.

John Lloyd Stephens and Frederick Catherwood visited the cenote at Bolonchén, or Nine Wells, located in the state of Campeche on the western edge of the Yucatán Peninsula. Stephens described the scene as he encountered it with a group of Maya guides. The water lies some 450 feet (135 m) below the surface of the ground. In order to reach the water, Stephens and the others descended into the black hole using a ladder made of planks fastened together by ropes. The Maya used pine torches to light their way. After reaching the water, Stephens and the others filled earthen pots tied to their heads and backs before returning to the surface. Catherwood's lithograph captures the scene as Stephens described it.

In Tikal, residents collected rainwater as it ran off their roofs by building wells around their dwellings and sacred buildings. To prevent losing the water to evaporation during hot weather, the Maya built roofs over the wells to protect the water.

The Maya also made use of reservoirs. For instance, the city of Tikal was located in a place with no rivers, lakes, or cenotes nearby. To compensate, residents built two large reservoirs to collect and store as much of the annual rainfall as possible. Maya workers used clay to line two natural ravines to form a watertight reservoir. City designers also built the main plaza with a slight slope (about 5 degrees), allowing all rainwater to flow naturally into the reservoirs. To keep the water from flowing out, builders constructed a boardwalk at one end, acting as a dam and providing a walkway for residents to cross the water.

Maya
Innovations

Throughout Mesoamerica, Maya cities spread with seemingly little fore-thought to location. Instead, it appears that the Maya simply built their cities wherever they happened to be settled. The local landscape caused the Maya to adapt accordingly. Consequently, Maya architecture often incorporates natural features within a specific location. For example, Maya living in the hills used and mimicked the hills by building tall temples on top of the hills. Thus, Maya cities in the hills displayed holy shrines towering into the sky. On the other hand, Maya living on the northern Yucatán plains did not build up. Instead, they built out, resulting in an extensive network of buildings and houses spread out over a large land area. The Maya on the plains literally built large, sprawling cities.

CITY PLANNING

There were some methods that dictated some aspects of almost every city. For instance, careful forethought was given to the location of important buildings in relation to one another and within the city. In particular, observatories and temples were situated based upon Maya reading of the stars. Maya priests analyzed the stars to determine where to construct the important buildings. Since all other buildings eventually grew out from the central plaza, usually located next to the central pyramid temple, the location for these buildings was an important detail.

Maya cities display both reasoned forethought and confused random-ness. On one hand, Maya cities often have the features of urban centers that require planning, such as large walkways, access to freshwater, and large public plazas. Each of these represents massive public works projects. In the case of securing freshwater, the Maya usually accomplished this important and necessary task by constructing aqueducts, reservoirs, or access to cenotes. These kinds of construction projects require planning. However, over time, most Maya cities continued to grow and remodel or build onto existing structures. Thus, instead of an orderly, well-planned city, Maya cities often looked like a collection of large buildings, temples, and causeways laid out in an arbitrary fashion.

In the center of the city lay the large plaza. Encircling the plaza were temples, palaces, and ball courts, all of which were symbols of royal and religious authority. The most ornate and largest buildings were located closest to the central plaza. Within this sphere lived the ruling class, priests, and upper nobility. Forming a ring around these buildings were the less important and smaller holy places commemorating minor nobles and lesser gods, as well as homes for those belonging to the lower nobility class. Beyond this sphere were the homes of the ordinary Maya.

During the Classic Period, Maya urban planning consisted of great monuments and large causeways. Planning seemingly focused on creating central plazas as gathering places for the local population. The inclusion of wide causeways, which provided easy access to the central squares, further emphasizes the focus on these central gathering places. Conversely, the inside of buildings often had little usable space. Instead, architectural planning favored the large, open public spaces over the private, interior space of homes. In addition, Maya architecture and urban planning did not place much weight on defensive fortifications. This is probably due to the Maya style of warfare, which did not stress capturing cities or locations, but people. Thus, Maya architecture of the Classic Period reflected the cultural attitudes and practices of the people.

BUILDING MATERIALS

The Maya used limestone more than any other material in building their great pyramids and cities in the jungles of Central America. The material was abundant and mined from locations nearby most cities. Limestone offered the advantage of being softer and more malleable when first taken from the quarry. Limestone hardens only after being quarried, which allowed the Maya to shape it and use it for construction projects. Each project only became more hardened over time.

The Maya also used a mortar made of crushed limestone, similar to cement. This mortar also served as the basis of stucco, a kind of mortar that is often used as a decorative finish to stonework. Although mortar was a component in some kinds of Maya houses, most consisted of wooden posts with thatch and adobe making up the bulk of the walls and roof. Wealthier citizens and those belonging to nobility sometimes enjoyed the luxuries of limestone houses.

Amazingly, the Maya did not have sophisticated technologies usually required for constructing large stone buildings and monuments. Indeed, these jungle dwellers lacked even the most basic forms of transporting heavy stone, such as horses or other animals to pull wagons or carts. In addition, the Maya did not have pulleys to leverage large stones, nor did they have metal tools to fashion it. Instead, this Mesoamerican civilization used the one key resource it did not lack: a large workforce.

PYRAMIDS

Perhaps the object most identified with the ancient Maya is the distinctive pyramid. Deep in the jungles of Central America remain these tall stone temples, reminders of an advanced people who no longer rule in these large, abandoned cities. Cut stonework adorns these stone structures, offering a glimpse into the past. The elaborate stone decorations provide researchers with important clues in understanding the Maya and the way they lived.

The pyramids constructed by the Maya had a few distinct characteristics. First, Maya pyramids were usually built using earth and stone rubble to form the core. Then, workers leveled the top, forming a platform. Cut limestone was placed on the facing, giving the artificial mound a finished look. At most sites, either one large stairway or four stairways—one on each side—led to the platform. At the manufactured high point, builders constructed one or more buildings. At some locations, there are several buildings on the platform. Archaeologists call a collection of these buildings an acropolis, which means the high point of a city.

Each succeeding generation added to existing platforms by enclosing existing buildings and constructing new platforms over the old. Then, a new temple or revered building would be constructed on the new platform, on top of the older one. Over time, the pyramids grew taller and narrower at the summit.

The most famous Mayan structures were the impressive pyramids, but most Maya lived in smaller, more humble structures of wooden posts and thatch and stucco walls. Those with higher social standing lived in fancier limestone houses.

During the Classic Period, Maya builders usually used the corbeled vault. This feature, which supported the roof, is often called the false arch. In a true arch, builders use a keystone at the uppermost point of the arch. The keystone actually holds the arch together, making the arch stronger. The keystone helps distribute the weight of the arch throughout all the stones of the arch, allowing the arch to have an arced or rounded look. In contrast, the corbeled vault resembles an upside-down V. To construct this false arch, builders lay stones one on top of the other, so that each hung slightly over the side of the one below it. This process was repeated on both sides until finally a single stone could connect the two sides. The result was an archlike roof or entryway with a high ceiling. This is a common feature in Maya architecture.

Buildings constructed using the corbeled vault required thick walls to support the weight of the stones in the false arch. To bear the weight, builders often used earth and rubble to make thick walls, then faced the walls with cut stone—much like the platforms themselves. Due to the thick walls and use of the corbeled vault, Maya buildings often look large on the outside, with little useable space on the inside.

OBSERVATORIES

El Castillo also boasts another feature, one that occurs twice each year. During both the spring and autumn solar equinoxes, the corner edge of the pyramid casts a shadow on the outer facing of center stairs. Due to the sloped edges of the corners, the shadow appears as a snake. Visitors flock from around the world to witness the so-called snake as it is revealed by the sun, the pyramid's shadow, and the ancient Maya knowledge that constructed the building to exhibit such a spectacle.

There is a small window at another location within El Castillo, at which observers see Venus only through that window. Remarkably, this occurrence happens only once every eight years.

The ancient Maya studied the sun and other stars as they moved across the sky. At Chichén Itzá are the remains of a round building known as the Caracol, which scholars believe was an observatory. Indeed, the ruins of this building resemble a modern observatory. Although the ancient structure did not accommodate a telescope, it was apparently used to observe the sun, stars, and other objects in the sky. Some of the windows within the Caracol face important celestial events. For instance, some windows face the sunset that corresponds to the spring and autumn equinox. Others align with Venus on its northernmost and southernmost position in the sky.

At Caracol is a grand staircase that appears to be out of alignment with other buildings at Chichén Itzá. The grand staircase faces 27.5 degrees north of west, virtually a perfect configuration to match the northernmost position of Venus in the sky. The building is also situated so that its northeast and southwest corners line up with the summer solstice sunrise and the winter solstice sunset. At the top of the grand staircase is another tower, now in ruins. This tower was smaller than the larger one on which it once sat. In order to ascend into the upper tower, one had to walk through a narrow, winding corridor that contained a staircase. The observatory is named for this staircase, El Caracol, or "snail" (or "spiral"), because of the winding path of these stairs.

The Maya observed and paid special attention to the planet Venus. There were several reasons for this interest. First, the Maya believed the planet to be the god of war and the evil twin of the sun. The Maya often planned battles and raids on their enemies based on the location of Venus. Second, the planet appears in both the evening and morning skies. This unique characteristic caused many other cultures to mistake Venus for a star, but the Maya knew Venus was a planet. Unlike many other cultures, the Maya also understood that Venus appeared both in the evening and in the morning.

Venus follows a steady and predictable pattern of appearance in the sky, both in the morning and evening. At the beginning of its cycle,

The great limestone pyramids of Maya civilization were built in the center of major cities and were used for religious and scientific purposes. Above, one of the most famous Maya pyramids, El Castillo, is located in Chichén Itzá.

Venus first appears at daybreak on the horizon. Each day following, the planet rises a little earlier and a little higher. Thus, Venus appears a little brighter each day in the morning sky. Once it reaches its apex, the cycle reverses itself and Venus begins to rise a little later each day, appearing a little lower in the sky, until finally it is not seen in the morning sky. This cycle, the rise and fall of Venus as a morning star, lasts 263 days. Then, for 50 days, Venus seemingly disappears altogether and is not seen in the sky at all.

At the end of the 50 days, Venus then reappears, but this time it is in the evening sky. The planet then enters another 263-day period mirroring the morning pattern. Thus, Venus rises a little earlier and higher each day, allowing it to shine more brightly than the night before, until it reaches its zenith and then moves in the opposite direction. At the end of the 263 days, the planet disappears again. However, when the evening Venus disappears on the horizon, it reappears in only 8 days. When Venus again shows itself, it is in the morning sky and the process starts anew. This entire cycle lasts for 584 days: 263 days as a morning star, unseen for 50 days, 263 days as an evening star, then unseen for 8 days. This cycle is also known as the synodic period of Venus.

Another unique curiosity to the synodic period of Venus is its relationship to the Earth's orbital period of 365 days. Five synodic periods of Venus equal eight Earth years; or the two have a 5:8 ratio relationship. Thus, five full Venus cycles always equal eight years. The Maya of long ago understood this and knew how to tell the passage of time using this astronomical cycle.

Much like the sun, the position of Venus shifts northward during the summer and southward during the winter. The exact position of the planet depends upon where it is within its cycle. The Maya observed that Venus completed this cycle once every eight years. The northern extreme and the southern extreme are the outermost points in this back-and-forth fluctuation of Venus in the sky.

In Maya beliefs, religion and science were both held in high regard, and they were intertwined with each other. Religious rituals flowed from what they knew about astronomy. Their understandings of astronomy fueled their advancements in and understandings of mathematics. Through their knowledge, the Maya could even accurately predict solar eclipses.

The Maya were expert astronomers and their religious beliefs were closely linked to movements in the night sky. Observatories, such as El Caracol in Chichén Itzá, did not have telescopes but were ideal spaces for ancient scientists to study the stars.

CALENDARS

The Maya used two different calendar systems, one astronomical and the other ceremonial. The astronomical calendar was based on the solar year. Called the *haab*, this calendar included 18 months, each 20 days long, which was a total of 360 days. Because the solar year, the time it takes for the Earth to complete its circle around the sun, is actually 365¼ days long, the Maya viewed the extra 5 days at the end of the year as unlucky because

THE MAYA CALENDAR AND THE END OF THE WORLD?

The Maya primarily used two different calendars, one for religious purposes and the other to mark the solar year. One shortcoming to the Maya methods was that their calendars followed a 52-year cycle. At the conclusion of a cycle, the terminology for dates repeated itself. Thus, a Maya native who lived into his or her fifties or sixties faced the confusing prospect of two sets of dates with the same names within his or her lifetime. Think of it his way: what if our calendar, including years, only went up to the year 52, then repeated itself over and over? That is what the Maya calendar system did.

To make up for this limitation, the Maya devised the Long Count calendar. The Maya developed the Long Count calendar in the first century B.C., long before the modern world adopted its current calendar. The Maya Long Count calendar begins recorded time in August 3114 B.C. Under Maya beliefs, this marks the beginning of the present great cycle, or the Maya fourth creation. Effectively, this date is the year zero for the Maya. At the conclusion of its 5,130-year great cycle, some argue that the Maya believe that the world will end. The last date on the Maya calendar is the winter solstice (December 21) of 2012. Proponents of this view point to the absence of a calendar beyond this date. Others challenge this view.

Does the Maya calendar really predict the end of the world? It does not seem likely, for the following reasons. First, there are many events detailed in the Popol Vuh that predate the year 3114 B.C. Thus, it does not appear that the calendars were intended to be the record for the beginning of time until the end of the world. Second, the Maya calendar also indicates dates well past 2012, such as a royal anniversary in October of A.D. 4772. Marking a future date is reasonable only if those marking the date expect the world to exist. Finally, it seems more likely that the winter solstice of 2012 marks the end of an old cycle and the beginning of a new one. Since each cycle lasts for over 5,000 years, it makes sense that

(continues)

(continued)

the Maya did not see the need to plan for more than one cycle at a time.

Despite these evidences, some still point to the last date on the Maya calendar as the end of the world. Such claims might be real, or they might be overly superstitious or the work of those sensationalizing something that few understand. Regardless, the attention these contemporary interpretations receive further highlights the intricacies and detailed accuracy of the ancient Maya as seen through their elaborate calendar systems.

they were not part of any month. This calendar had one major flaw: Since the solar calendar had an additional quarter day, the Maya haab would lose days over time. However, the calendar was extremely advanced for ancient peoples. Indeed, the haab was the most advanced and accurate calendar used by ancient civilizations. The second calendar system was the *tzolkin*. This calendar had only 260 days, each of which was a sacred day for the Maya. The tzolkin reminded the Maya when to worship deities, celebrate important anniversaries, and commemorate past leaders. Thus, the haab acted as the calendar for everyday life, while the tzolkin served as the religious calendar.

The ancient Maya carved the two calendars onto round stone disks. Then, they placed the two disks next to each other and rotated the disks. Solar days were thus matched to holy days. Which holy day from the tzolkin lined up with the corresponding day on the haab determined whether a day was considered lucky or unlucky.

The Maya methods appear overly complex. The process of determining the date required knowledge and understanding. Priests held this knowledge, giving them influence and authority within society. All members of a Maya city-state, from the ruler down to the poorest peasant, relied upon the calendars. The calendar system revealed things such as when to plan crops and when to harvest, when to begin or celebrate the completion of a building project, and which days were good for going to war or forming a marriage. The intricacies of the calendar system empowered the priests, who held the key to unlocking the secrets of the calendar wheels.

MAYA MATHEMATICS

The Maya developed a system for counting using only three symbols: a symbol for zero, a dot, and a bar. Though relatively simple, this system allowed its users to count and record very large numbers. The symbol for zero (or completion) was usually a shell.

Their system differed from ours in two distinct ways. First, their numbering system used a base of 20, as opposed to 10. (A system with a base of 10 is called a decimal system, while the Maya system with a base of 20 is called a vigesimal system.) Thus, instead of the digit in the second position from the right having a value 10 times the digit in the first position, the second digit had a value 20 times that in the first position. Then, the digit in the third position was not 100 times the value of the first, but 400 times (not 10 x 10, but 20 x 20), and so on. The second major difference was that the place values were arranged vertically, rather than horizontally.

Advantages to this numbering system included the ability to record dates and years accurately, something that held great importance to the Maya as they watched and predicted the paths of the sun, the moon, and Venus. The Maya calendar was also based on 20, with both the solar and ceremonial calendars consisting of months with 20 days. It is impossible to determine whether the math system led to the development of the calendars or if the calendars influenced the development of their mathematic system. Regardless, the two systems are closely linked, and both rely on the base of 20. Scholars are uncertain if the Maya ever developed a means of multiplication or division for their numbering system.

Learning
About the Maya

Researchers today have learned many things about the ancient Maya. Most of what is known has been deciphered from hieroglyphic carvings on stelae, temples, or other Maya structures. Although archaeologists and historians have learned a great deal about the Maya, there are also large gaps in the historical record, making it difficult to understand more fully the early inhabitants of that great Mesoamerican civilization.

Other than stone carvings, modern researchers do not have very many Mayan writings that survive today. Spanish explorers first made contact with the Maya in 1502. Fifteen years later, Spanish settlers began making inroads into Maya territory. In 1524, the Spanish conquest of the Maya began, culminating in the European power dominating the territory of the ancient civilization. For the native peoples, the result of these interactions with the Spanish was the destruction of many Mayan records.

UNDERSTANDING MAYAN CARVINGS

Written language is one of the key traits historians seek when evaluating the degree to which culture is civilized versus unsophisticated. In the case of the Maya, their writings stand alone in the pre-Columbian times of the New World. No other civilization in the New World invented their own writing. Indeed, later cultures borrowed heavily from the Maya and their writing. Much of the writing that survives is found in pyramids, stelae, and other stonework carved by Maya artisans hundreds of years before Columbus first sailed to the New World. Today, hieroglyphic carvings are one of the most distinctive and unique features of Maya culture.

Archaeologists have learned a great deal about Maya life, culture, and society from carved glyphs found on stonework and the pyramids. The Maya civilization stands out from other New World civilizations because it is the only one that developed a written language.

In all civilizations around the world, writing takes place in three distinct phases of development: pictorial (or representative) writing, ideographic writing, and phonetic writing. In pictorial writing, images or pictures represent an idea. In contrast, a character represents an idea in ideographic writing. Finally, characters in phonetic writing represent sounds, not an idea. Mayan writing falls into the second stage, or ideographic writing, since most Mayan characters stand for an idea as opposed to pictures or sounds. However, there is some evidence that at least some Mayan characters exhibit some elements of phonetic writing, meaning the characters might represent sounds as well as an idea.

When the Spanish established control over the Yucatán in the late seventeenth century, local Maya still used hieroglyphic writing. Although the Maya civilization had declined around A.D. 900, understanding of hieroglyphics and the expertise to pass that knowledge on continued to survive. The wealthier and upper-class Maya, especially the priests and ruling class, continued to read and write using the traditional Maya methods. Bishop Diego de Landa recorded much of what is now known about the hieroglyphs. In his 1566 book, *Relación de las cosas de Yucatán*, Landa described the Maya calendar systems, including drawings of various signs and their meaning. Landa learned about the Maya calendar from a Maya prince named Nachi Cocum, who was knowledgeable in hieroglyphs. Landa viewed Mayan writings as evil and later attempted to do away with all paper copies he could find. Amazingly, this same bishop also provided modern researchers with one of their most valuable resources. Landa endeavored to produce a phonetic rendering of Mayan glyphs, using the Latin alphabet. In other words, Landa tried to translate Mayan pictures into Latin letters so others could better understand the meanings of the pictures. Although his work was incomplete, it has served as the foundation from which some Mayan hieroglyphs can be understood.

John Lloyd Stephens understood that the hieroglyphs were the key to understanding the Maya. He guessed the glyphs contained historical records of the ancient people. Although he could not read the glyphs, Stephens's hunch as to the importance of the stone records was correct. The Maya recorded key dates and events in stone. Stephens tried to preserve what he could of the Maya civilization, mostly through Catherwood's lithographs. In other instances, Stephens—as well as other early researchers—removed objects from the ruins in order to study them.

MAKING MAYA PAPER

The Maya began making paper during the early Classic Period, perhaps as early as the mid-third century. This paper was made from the inner bark of a wild fig tree, the ficus. The Maya who lived in the lowlands, where this kind of fig tree is common, called the ficus *hu'un*, or *hun*. This is the same word the ancient Maya used for paper and the books they made from this paper. No firsthand account of Maya paper production exists, but scholars do know how the Aztec made paper. Descendants of the Maya still make paper from inner tree bark, and the processes mimic those of the Aztec. Historian Michael Coe argues in *The Art of the Maya Scribe* that ancient Maya paper-making closely resembles that of the Aztec and modern Maya. The process, described by Coe, includes six steps.

The fig branches are collected. These branches are longer than 5 feet (1.5 meters) long and about 1 inch (25 millimeters) in diameter.

The branches are cut lengthwise in order to remove the bark— both the inner and outer bark—in one piece.

The outer bark is removed from the strips and then the inner bark is soaked in running water. During this step, the latex, which is present in all species of ficus, thickens and is then removed by scraping the congealed mass from the inner bark.

The bark fibers are dried. Then, taking the water leftover from soaking corn in lime and water, along with lye or more lime, the bark fibers are boiled.

The fibers are now soft and flexible. They are removed from the mixture and rinsed in cold water before being placed in a large pot or gourd.

The processed fibers are cut to fit into a wooden drying boar, which has a flat surface. The fibers are laid in the following configuration: one set of fibers is laid lengthwise; the next set is laid widthwise. In order to bind the layers together, the fibers are pounded down. In this way, the separate layers become a single piece of usable paper.

Sometimes, efforts to preserve and understand the Maya civilization have resulted in lost knowledge. For example, John Lloyd Stephens visited Uxmal in 1840–1841. While there, he investigated one of the most stunning buildings in Mesoamerica from the pre-Columbian era, the Governor's Palace. In this building, Stephens discovered a carved sapodilla beam. Stephens claimed it was the only carved piece of timber at the site. When he left Yucatán, Stephens took the timber with him. The inscription possibly held the key to dating the palace. Unfortunately, the beam was lost forever when it was consumed in a fire in New York City.

LOST HISTORY

A key figure in understanding what Maya history is known and what Maya history is lost to us today is that of a sixteenth-century Franciscan friar. Diego de Landa arrived on the Yucatán Peninsula in 1549. Landa sought to end Maya religious ceremonies and traditions. The priest also wanted to convert the Maya to Roman Catholicism. In order to accomplish this, Landa took drastic measures. First, he rounded up many of the Maya priests. These poor souls faced torture at the hands of the overzealous Landa, who sought to change the minds of the Maya priests, then of the Maya nobility, to accept Roman Catholicism.

Next, Landa set out to destroy the written records of the Maya. Each codex was a colorful folding book made of bark cloth that contained Mayan hieroglyphic text. These codices contained the recorded history and beliefs of the Maya. They remained in existence in large numbers until Landa ordered their destruction in July 1562. At that time, at least 40 codices were burned, as well as thousands of idols. Throughout the remaining years of Spanish conquest in Maya territory, officials usually seized and burned codices whenever discovered. Unfortunately, these records contained much of the history of the Maya from the end of the Classic Period to the time of the Spanish arrival. The codices might have held clues for learning about the Maya collapse. However, whatever knowledge was contained within the codices is largely gone forever.

Today, only four Maya manuscripts survive. These folding books are called the Dresden Codex, the Madrid Codex, the Paris Codex, and the Grolier Codex. The first three are named after the cities in which they currently reside. These are believed to be complete works of varying lengths. Of the three, the Dresden Codex is considered the most important for its

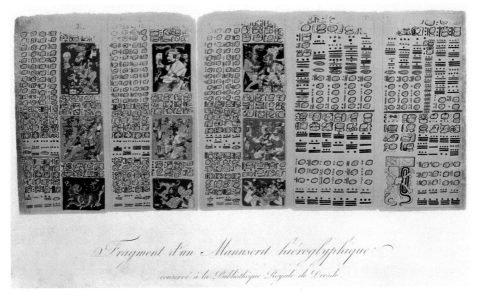

Fragment d'un Manuscrit hiéroglyphique conservé à la Bibliothèque Royale de Dresde.

In their zeal to convert the Maya to Roman Catholicism, Spanish missionaries tortured Maya priests and destroyed codices that documented the civilization's history and religious beliefs. Only four of these precious texts survived this purge, one of which is known as the Dresden Codex.

content and artistic qualities. This codex also contains information about the cycles of Venus (six pages) and eclipses, as well as ritualistic references. Written on a book of 39 folding leaves, the Dresden Codex is actually a long sheet of paper with writing on both sides. Scholars believe this codex was written just prior to the Spanish conquest. There is no record of how it ended up in Europe, until the royal library of Saxony, located in Dresden, purchased the codex in 1739. An exact replica of the Dresden Codex has been on display since 2007 at the national museum in Guatemala City.

The Madrid Codex is not as elaborate or decorative as the Dresden Codex, but it is longer, containing 112 pages. This work was probably written after the Spanish first arrived in the New World. The content appears to be a collection of other texts, so the work may have been an attempt to save important Maya knowledge in one book. Believed to originate from the Maya city of Tayasal, it is possible that Hernando Cortés acquired the codex and sent it to Spanish authorities. On two separate occasions, the book was divided into two sections (Troano Codex and Cortésianus Codex). The two portions were finally reunited in 1888.

The Paris Codex first appeared in the National Library of France in 1832. A reproduction of the 22-page codex was completed in 1835. Unfortunately, only a small portion of the original survives. Were it not for the copy, this codex would be lost. The copy was misplaced and forgotten until 1859, when it was found in a basket full of papers in a corner chimney, which explains the poor condition of the codex. The Paris Codex includes the equivalent of the Maya zodiac and Maya prophecies related to their calendar.

In contrast to the other three codices, the Grolier Codex is a fragment of just 11 pages of a longer codex, which is why this one is sometimes called the Grolier Fragment. The Grolier Codex came to light in the 1970s and is held in a museum in Mexico. It does not provide any details not already contained in the Dresden Codex. In addition, the artwork in this codex is of poorer quality than the other surviving documents. The authenticity of the Grolier Codex remains in question.

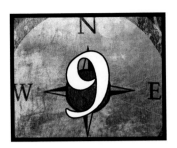

The
Maya Legacy

Today there are millions of Maya descendants living in Mesoamerica. Modern Maya live in the region that still contains the stone ruins of the ancient civilization. Among them are the Lacandon, a group numbering about 500 people dwelling in the Yucatán. The Lacandon live in Chiapas, a state in Mexico. This small group of Maya live within three small villages (two in the north and one in the south), living in many of the traditional ways near the ruins of Palenque and Yaxchilan. There are two distinctive groups of Lacandon. Those in the north avoid conflict and embrace peaceful coexistence, whereas those in the south tend to protect their identity—through violence when necessary.

Like their ancestors, the Lacandon Maya practice slash-and-burn agriculture as well as hunting and gathering for their food sources. In addition, some work for wages while others sell crafts and other authentically made items to tourists. Researchers believe that this group speaks a dialect of Yucatac Mayan. In their native tongue, members of the group call themselves the "true people." Researchers believe that the Lacandon ancestors fled from the Spanish in the seventeenth century, finding refuge in the jungles of the Yucatán. There was little contact between these Maya and the outside world for over 200 years. Researchers became aware of their existence in the early twentieth century. Since the Spanish never successfully colonized this group of Maya, they are indeed descendants of the actual Maya, though some evidence suggests that the Spanish and other Maya groups might have influenced the Lacandon over the past several hundred years. The Lacandon lived in relative isolation from the rest of Mexican society until recent decades. Thus, this group has preserved many traits of the pre-Hispanic Maya culture. The Hispanic culture has absorbed most of the other Maya peoples in the region. Despite their isolation, the Lacandon Maya have slowly accepted some of the Mexican ways since the mid-twentieth century, taking on more and more of the Hispanic cultural traits.

In addition to practicing the slash-and-burn agricultural techniques of their forbearers, the Lacandon rely on maize as their primary agricultural crop. Until recent decades, this group continued to hunt game with bow and arrow. Since the Lacandon had such low populations, their practices did not disrupt the ecological balance in their territory. However, the introduction of more modern hunting methods and weapons by other residents in the area has upset that balance and forced the Lacandon to seek more contact with the outside world in order to survive, such as engaging in trade with tourists. Beginning in the 1960s, peasants seeking food have migrated into Lacandon territory, devastating the food sources of this small clan of Maya. In the early 1970s, the Mexican government allotted the Lacandon a portion of the profits made from opening the rain forest up to logging. The results of these actions have led to the rapid adoption of Hispanic culture into the Lacandon way of life. Modern conveniences and technologies, school, tin-roofed houses, and automobiles are now a part of modern Lacandon life.

The Lacandon still wear the traditional dress of their ancestors, but this is done only near the Palenque ruins as a means to attract the attention of tourists in the hopes they will purchase Lacandon handmade weapons. When the tourists are not present, many of the Lacandon favor modern clothing.

Other aspects of Lacandon identity have also eroded in recent years. For instance, most Lacandon still practiced a form of the ancient Maya religion until just 60 years ago. Many of the Lacandon have converted to Christian denominations, especially Seventh-Day Adventism. A small minority still practice the old religious rites. Most that adhere to the Maya religious practices live in the northern village of Laja. As in the Classic Period, these practices form the basis of community life and center around the temple. However, the Lacandon temples are humble shacks made of thatch compared with the grand pyramids that still stand. Most rites involve a small sacrifice of food or incense and the drinking of *balche*, an alcoholic drink.

Modern Maya still live in the region that was once occupied by their ancestors. Although many have converted to Christianity or have adopted a more modern lifestyle, there is still a small minority that practice traditional Maya beliefs.

One of the most distinctive cultural traits retained by the Lacandon is their language. The Maya still speak traditional dialects of their native tongue, as well as Spanish. Another commonality that many modern Maya share with their ancestors is reliance on the agricultural crop that their ancestors ate: corn.

RECENT MAYA ARCHAEOLOGY AND DISCOVERIES

Maya lands continue to be a rich source of interest to archaeologists and researchers. Recent discoveries reveal some interesting things about water at Palenque. Archaeologists have discovered a set of narrowing aqueduct channels in the southern urban center. This discovery means the Maya understood enough about water pressure to create fountains, which is where the channels lead. Palenque included an elaborate system for catching rainwater and draining water away from the public plazas. The presence of water pressure to fill water jugs or for a fountain is remarkable. The finding is the first of its kind in Mesoamerican civilizations. Its discovery has ramifications for researchers of other Mesoamerican civilizations, causing them to reexamine some of the water and drainage systems in other sites.

AN ARCHAEOLOGICAL HERITAGE

The accomplishments of the ancient Maya in the area of construction projects are difficult to overlook. The abandoned cities, even though they stood in ruins, deeply impressed the Spanish explorers of the sixteenth century when they first encountered the once-great but crumbling urban centers. Remnants of their great cities still stand. Temple pyramids still rise up in the rain forests of Central America. These stone edifices stand as a tribute to the ingenuity and technical knowledge of the Maya.

ASTRONOMY

The Maya watched the heavens and recorded their observations. Many of their records, engraved in stone, still survive. These observations demonstrate that the Maya accurately understood and predicted the cycles of the sun, the moon, and Venus. These observations also enabled the Maya to measure time in precise ways.

MAIZE

Perhaps the most enduring Maya legacy is that of maize. Today, corn is produced in more countries than any other crop. It has proved to be an adaptable plant, making it possible to raise it nearly anywhere, from hot and dry environments to cold and wet climates. Corn is perhaps one of the most important food sources in the entire world. In terms of value and volume, it is easily the largest for the United States, the world leader in agricultural production. Furthermore, the United States produces more corn than any other country, raising nearly 40 percent of the world's annual corn production. The Great Plains in the midwestern United States offer some of the best conditions for producing corn.

Of what use is the crop of the ancient Maya to the modern world? Corn is an important source of food for animals and humans. It is used in livestock feed, human food, and sweeteners. In addition to its food value, corn is also raised to produce fuel. The increasing use of ethanol in recent years has spurred even greater emphasis on raising corn, especially as the cost of oil has risen.

There are primarily three classifications of corn today: dent, flint, and sweet. Dent corn, frequently called field corn, is most commonly used as feed for livestock. Dent corn is raised in both yellow and white varieties. This is also the kind of corn used in processed foods and for industrial products. Another kind of corn is flint. A hard outer shell and colorful kernels characterize flint corn, often called Indian corn. Central and South America produce most of the world's flint corn. One form of flint corn is popcorn. Popcorn possesses a center within the hard-shelled kernel that is

The information gathered from Maya ruins proves that it was the most advanced civilization in the New World. Their unique contributions to astronomy, agriculture, math, and art have helped shape modern-day methods, and their ruins continue to tower over modern-day towns and cities.

soft and starchy. When heated, the moisture within the soft, starchy center becomes steam, which expands rapidly and finally causes the kernel to explode. The result is the familiar-looking white, fluffy, lightweight snack. Sweet corn is the third kind of corn. Sweet corn contains higher levels of natural sugars than other kinds of corn. Sweet corn is produced almost exclusively for human consumption. It is usually served fresh, often on the

THE MANY USES OF CORN

The ancient Maya did not know it, but their primary crop of maize, or corn, was one of the most versatile and amazing agricultural products ever discovered. Today, corn or some if its by-products are used in literally thousands of different products. Many processed foods, a characteristic of modern life, contain corn or corn derivatives. Below is a list of some of the many foods and products that use corn, as found at the Ontario Corn Producers' Association Web site (http://www.ontariocorn.org/classroom/products.html):

Adhesives

Aluminum

Antibiotics (penicillin)

Asbestos insulation

Aspirin

Baby food

Beer

Breakfast cereals

Candies

Canned vegetables

Carbonated beverages

Cheese spreads

Chewing gum

Chocolate products

Coatings on wood, paper, and metal

Color carrier in paper and textile printing

Cosmetics

Crayon and chalk

Degradable plastics

Dessert powders

Disposable diapers

Dyes

Edible oil

Ethyl and butyl alcohol

Explosives, firecrackers

Finished leather

cob, or preserved by canning or freezing methods. Producers rarely use sweet corn for livestock feed or processed products.

Other kinds of corn, called value enhanced, have been developed through research over time. These value-enhanced corns are grown in order to boost certain qualities, such as increased nutritional content or higher concentrations of oil or starch.

Flour and grits

Fructose

Fuel ethanol

Gypsum wallboard

Ink for stamping prices in stores

Insecticides

Instant coffee and tea

Insulation, fiberglass

Jams, jellies, and preserves

Ketchup

Latex paint

Leather tanning

Licorice

Livestock feed

Malted products

Margarine

Mayonnaise

Mustard, prepared

Paper board (corrugating, laminating, cardboard)

Paper manufacturing

Paper plates and cups

Peanut butter

Potato chips

Rugs and carpets

Salad dressings

Shaving cream and lotions

Shoe polish

Soaps and cleaners

Soft drinks

Starch and glucose (over 40 types)

Syrup

Textiles

Toothpaste

Wallpaper

Wheat bread

Whiskey

Yogurts

Corn or by-products of processed corn are used in literally hundreds of different items, such as soaps, adhesives, dyes, paint, and many others. There is even a biodegradable corn plastic! Corn, especially its sugar and/or starch, is also a component in many human foods. In addition, the corn plant is one of the most studied plants, serving as the primary study plant for biochemistry, genetics, agricultural studies, and soil fertility.

LEGACY

In many respects, the Maya civilization of the Classic Period is gone. However, there are relics that still survive, reminding world citizens in the twenty-first century of a long-gone culture that began, flourished, and died out more than 1,100 years ago. The Maya reached their height and had already begun to decline more than three centuries before England's King John signed the Magna Carta. The Maya had already abandoned many of their cities some 600 years before Christopher Columbus set sail for the New World. The most advanced of the pre-Columbian American cultures was already past its zenith before Europeans even knew it existed. Yet their achievements in astronomy and mathematics, their expertise in construction, and their beliefs are now known and appreciated around the world.

Chronology

2500 B.C.– **A.D. 250**	Preclassic Period
A.D. 250–900	Classic Period
900–1500	Postclassic Period
426	The first dynasty at Copán is established by K'inich Yax K'uk'Mo
683	Palenque's ruler, Pakal the Great, dies and is buried in the Temple of Inscriptions
749–763	Smoke Shell rules Copán and constructs the Temple of the Hieroglyphic Stairway
1502	During his fourth and final voyage to the New World, Christopher Columbus becomes the first European to meet Maya natives
1517	The Spanish begin to penetrate into Maya territory
1524	Spanish conquistador Pedro de Alvarado conquers the Maya in Guatemala
1528	Hernando Cortés takes cacao beans to Spain, introducing the ancient drink to Europe
1697	Martín de Ursúa, Spanish governor of Yucatán, captures the last free Maya city of Tayasal, cementing Spanish rule over Maya territory
1821	Mexico gains its independence from Spain. The Yucatán Peninsula, the territory of the Maya, becomes part of Mexico
1839	John Lloyd Stephens and artist Frederick Catherwood rediscover the Maya civilization
1841	John Lloyd Stephens publishes *Incidents of Travel in Central America, Chiapas, and Yucatan*, detailing his discoveries of the Maya
2012	The date some believe the Maya calendars indicate will be the end of the world

Timeline

683
Palenque's ruler, Pakal the Great, dies and is buried in the Temple of Inscriptions

1697
Martín de Ursúa, Spanish governor of Yucatán, captures the last free Maya city of Tayasal, cementing Spanish rule over Maya territory

683

1697

1517
The Spanish begin to penetrate into Maya territory

1839
John Lloyd
Stephens and
artist Frederick
Catherwood
rediscover the
Maya civilization

1821

2012

1821
Mexico gains its
independence from
Spain. The Yucatán
Peninsula, the ter-
ritory of the Maya,
becomes part of
❖ Mexico

2012
The date some
believe the Maya
calendars indicate
will be the end of
the world ❖

Glossary

aqueduct   A human-made structure or channel that allows water to move from one location to another.

archaeologist   A researcher who studies ancient people and their culture.

astrologer   Someone who studies the heavens and celestial objects in an attempt to understand and predict human events.

astronomical   Relating to astronomy, the study of the heavens.

ceiba   A large tree that grows in the tropics and has large pods.

cenote   A natural, deep well in limestone that is filled with groundwater.

ceramic   A hard, breakable material made from baking clay, usually used for pottery or other dishes.

Chac   The Maya rain god.

chisel   A metal tool used to carve or shape wood, stone, or metal.

codex   An ancient manuscript, usually made of bark paper (plural: codices).

dibble stick   A pointed stick used by the Maya to make holes in the soil for planting seeds.

drought   An extended period of dry weather.

eclipse   The total or partial blocking of one celestial body by another, such as the moon blocking the sun (solar eclipse).

equinox   Two days each year when the length of day is equal to the length of night. In the Northern Hemisphere, the spring equinox occurs around March 21, and the fall equinox occurs around September 23.

flint   A hard stone.

glyph   Symbols or characters usually carved in relief.

hacienda   A large plantation.

hieroglyphs   Pictographic script in which many of the symbols are pictures of the ideas being represented.

Kukulkán   The plumed or feathered serpent god of the Maya (the Aztec god was called Quetzalcoatl).

Mesoamerica   The region in which several civilizations, including the Maya, flourished, extending approximately from central Mexico to Honduras and Nicaragua.

nomadic   A lifestyle of hunter-gatherer cultures in which the people have no permanent dwelling or settlement.

observatory   A building designed and used for making observations of astronomical, meteorological, or other natural cycles.

obsidian   A hard, volcanic glass used by the ancient Maya to fashion knives and other weapons and tools.

shroud   A garment used for burial.

solstice   The day each year when the sun reaches its extreme southern or northern position in the sky. In the Northern Hemisphere, the winter solstice occurs near December 21 (extreme southern position), and the summer solstice occurs near June 21 (extreme northern position).

stela   A stone pillar or slab (plural: stelae).

stucco   A material made from cement or plaster and used to decorate stone walls.

sundial   An instrument used to show the time of day, accomplished by viewing the shadow cast by the sun onto a fixed horizontal plate.

thong   A strip of leather.

urn   A large, decorative vase, usually for holding cremated remains.

Bibliography

Braswell, Geoffrey E., ed. *The Maya and Teotihuacan: Reinterpreting Early Classic Interaction*. Austin: University of Texas Press, 2003.

Coe, Michael D. *The Art of the Maya Scribe*. New York: Harry N. Abrams, 1997.

———. *The Maya*. 6th ed. New York: Thames & Hudson, 1999.

Culbert, T. Patrick, ed. *Classic Maya Collapse*. Albuquerque: University of New Mexico Press, 1977.

Demarest, Arthur Andrew. *Ancient Maya: The Rise and Fall of a Rainforest Civilization*. Cambridge, UK: Cambridge University Press, 2004.

Demarest, Arthur Andrew, Prudence M. Rice, and Don Stephen Rice. *The Terminal Classic in the Maya Lowlands: Collapse, Transition, and Transformation*. Boulder: University Press of Colorado, 2004.

Drew, David. *The Lost Chronicles of the Maya Kings*. New ed. London: Phoenix Press, 2004.

Freidel, David, and Linda Schele. *A Forest of Kings: The Untold Story of the Ancient Maya*. New York: Harper Collins, 1992.

Garber, James, ed. *The Ancient Maya of the Belize Valley: Half a Century of Archaeological Research*. Gainesville: University Press of Florida, 2004.

Grube, Nikolai. *Maya: Divine Kings of the Rainforest*. Konigswinter, Germany: H.F. Ullman, 2007.

Haughton, Brian. *Hidden History: Lost Civilizations, Secret Knowledge, and Ancient Mysteries*. Edison, N.J.: Castle Books, 2008.

Herring, Adam. *Art and Writing in the Maya Cities, A.D. 600–800: A Poetics of Line*. Cambridge, UK: Cambridge University Press, 2005.

Jordan, Shirley. *Mayan Civilization: Moments in History*. Logan, Iowa: Perfection Learning Corporation, 2001.

Landa, Diego de. *Yucatán Before and After the Conquest*. Translated by William Gates. New York: Dover Publications, 1978.

Lohse, Jon C., and Fred Valdez. *Ancient Maya Commoners*. Austin: University of Texas Press, 2004.

Love, Michael. "Recent Research in the Southern Highlands and Pacific Coast of Mesoamerica." *Journal of Archaeological Research* 15 (December 2007): 275–328.

Lucero, Lisa Joyce. *Water and Ritual: The Rise and Fall of Classic Maya Rulers*. Austin: University of Texas Press, 2006.

McKillop, Heather Irene. *In Search of Maya Sea Traders*. College Station: Texas A & M University Press, 2005.

———. *The Ancient Maya: New Perspectives*. New York: W.W. Norton & Company, 2006.

McNeil, Cameron L. *Chocolate in Mesoamerica: A Cultural History of Cacao*. Gainesville: University Press of Florida, 2006.

Menzies, Gavin. *1421: The Year China Discovered the New World*. New York: Harper Collins Publishers, 2003.

Miller, Mary, and Karl Taube. *The Gods and Symbols of Ancient Mexico and the Maya*. London: Thames & Hudson, 1993.

Morley, Sylvanus Griswold. *The Ancient Maya*. 3rd ed. Stanford, Calif.: Stanford University Press, 1946.

Pagden, A.R., trans. and ed. *Diego de Landa's Account of the Affairs of the Maya*. Chicago: J. Philip O'Hara, 1975.

Perl, Lila. *The Ancient Maya*. New York: Franklin Watts, 2005.

Peterson, Roger Tory, and Edward L. Chalif. *A Field Guide to Mexican Birds*. Boston: Houghton Mifflin, 1973.

Rice, Prudence M. *Maya Political Science: Time, Astronomy, and the Cosmos*. Austin: University of Texas Press, 2004.

Saunders, Nicholas J. *Icons of Power: Feline Symbolism in the Americas*. London: Routledge, 1998.

Schele, Linda, Mary Ellen Miller, and Justin Kerr. *The Blood of Kings: Dynasty and Ritual in Maya Art*. New York: George Braziller, 1986.

Sharer, Robert J. *Daily Life in Maya Civilization*. Santa Barbara, Calif.: Greenwood Press, 1996.

Sharer, Robert J., and Loa P. Traxler. *The Ancient Maya*. 6th ed. Stanford, Calif.: Stanford University Press, 2006.

Stephens, John L. *Incidents of Travel in Yucatán*. 2 vols. New York: Harper & Brothers, 1855.

Stuart, David, and George Stuart. *Palenque: Eternal City of the Maya*. London: Thames & Hudson, 2008.

Tedlock, Dennis. *Popol Vuh: The Definitive Edition of the Mayan Book of the Dawn of Life and the Glories of Gods and Kings*. New York: Simon & Schuster, 1985.

Tiesler, Vera, and Andrea Cucina. *Janaab' Pakal of Palenque: Reconstructing the Life and Death of a Maya Ruler*. Tucson: University of Arizona Press, 2006.

Webster, David L. *The Fall of the Ancient Maya*. London: Thames & Hudson, 2002.

Further Resources

Books

Beach, Rod. *Dusty Sandals: The Demise of the Mayan & Anasazi Civilization.* Parker, Colo.: Outskirts Press, 2006.

Christie, Jessica Joyce. *Maya Palaces and Elite Residences: An Interdisciplinary Approach.* Austin: University of Texas Press, 2003.

Coggins, Clemency, ed. *Artifacts from the Cenote of Sacrifice Chichen Itza, Yucatán: Textiles, Basketry, Stone, Shell, Ceramics, Wood, Copal, Rubber (Memoirs of the Peabody Museum).* Cambridge, Mass.: Harvard University Press, 1992.

McKillop, Heather Irene. *Salt: White Gold of the Ancient Maya.* Gainesville: University Press of Florida, 2002.

Web Sites

Authentic Maya
http://www.authenticmaya.com/ancient_guatemala.htm

"Chichén Itzá," Exploratorium
http://www.exploratorium.edu/ancientobs/chichen/HTML/castillo.html

"Courtly Art of the Ancient Maya: Life at the Maya Court," National Gallery of Art
http://www.nga.gov/exhibitions/2004/maya/lifeatcourt.shtm

"Courtly Art of the Ancient Maya: Numbers," National Gallery of Art
http://www.nga.gov/exhibitions/2004/maya/numbers.shtm

"Lost King of the Maya," NOVA Online
http://www.pbs.org/wgbh/nova/maya

"Maya Astronomy," Kuxan Suum
http://www.kuxansuum.net/page8.php

"The Maya: Death Empire," History Television
http://www.history.ca/ontv/titledetails.aspx?titleid=104664

Mayaweb
http://www.mayaweb.nl/enghome.htm

"Mesoamerica," Foundation for the Advancement of Mesoamerican Studies
http://www.famsi.org

Mike Ruggeri's Maya Archaeology News
http://web.me.com/michaelruggeri/Mike_Ruggeris_Maya_Archaeology_
News/Mike_Ruggeris_Maya_Archaeology_News.html

"NASA, University Scientists Uncover Lost Maya Ruins—from Space,"
   NASA
http://www.nasa.gov/centers/marshall/multimedia/photos/2006/
photos06-018.html

Pre-Columbian Maya
http://www.worldmuseumofman.org/mayan2.php

Picture Credits

Index

About the Author

DR. SHANE MOUNTJOY resides in York, Nebraska, where he is an associate professor of history and the vice president for student development/dean of students at York College. Mountjoy has received recognition from students and peers as an outstanding teacher. He has earned degrees from York College, Lubbock Christian University, the University of Nebraska, and the University of Missouri. He is the author of more than a dozen books and appears in the documentary *The Lost Civilizations of North America.*

Rock Music Library

Kurt Cobain

by Michael Martin

Consultant: Meredith Rutledge
Assistant Curator
Rock and Roll Hall of Fame and Museum
Cleveland, Ohio

Capstone
press

Mankato, Minnesota

Edge Books are published by Capstone Press
151 Good Counsel Drive, P.O. Box 669, Mankato, Minnesota 56002
www.capstonepress.com

Library of Congress Cataloging-in-Publication Data
Martin, Michael, 1948–
    Kurt Cobain / by Michael Martin.
    p. cm.—(Edge Books. Rock music library)
    Includes bibliographical references and index.
    ISBN 0-7368-2700-5 (hardcover)
    1. Cobain, Kurt, 1967–1994—Juvenile literature. 2. Rock musicians—United
States—Biography—Juvenile literature. [1. Cobain, Kurt, 1967–1994. 2. Musicians.
3. Rock music.] I. Title. II. Series.
ML3930.C525M37 2005
782.42166'092—dc22   2003026404

Summary: Traces the life, career, and impact of rock musician Kurt Cobain.

Editorial Credits
Angela Kaelberer, editor; Jason Knudson, series designer; Molly Nei, book designer;
    Jo Miller, photo researcher; Scott Thoms, photo editor; Eric Kudalis, product
    planning editor

Photo Credits
AP/Wide World Photos/Robert Sorbo, 5
Corbis/S.I.N./Ian Tilton, 9, 10, 12, 19; S.I.N./Martyn Goodacre, 23, 26;
    Corbis Sygma/Jay Blakesberg, 25
Getty Images Inc./Frank Micelotta, cover, 15; Myrna Suarez, 29
WireImage/James Crump, 21; Kevin Mazur, 6, 17, 24

Table of Contents

CHAPTER 1

Shock in Seattle

April 8, 1994, was a dark day for millions of rock music fans. Early that morning, a body was discovered in a house in Seattle, Washington. Rumors spread quickly. People said that Kurt Cobain had killed himself with a shotgun. Hours later, police said the rumors were true. Police used fingerprints to prove that the body was Kurt's.

Learn about:

Kurt's death

A troubled life

Music lives on

Police removed Kurt's body from his Seattle home on April 8, 1994.

Kurt's love for his wife and child was not enough to save him.

A Puzzling Life

Kurt's life was full of contradictions. He was talented, but he had little respect for his abilities. He said he did not want to be a rock star. Yet he worked hard to become famous. Millions of people loved his music. But he became upset when people told him they liked his work.

Kurt never seemed satisfied. At the time of his death, he was rich. He had fans all over the world. Other musicians wanted to work with him. He had a wife and a baby daughter whom he loved deeply. Still, Kurt was unhappy.

Kurt Cobain was one of the most remarkable people in rock history. He was only 27 years old when he died. His music and personality touched millions of people during his short life. Kurt's story is both fascinating and tragic. It's also hard to understand. The best place to start is the small town where he grew up.

CHAPTER 2

Music in the Blood

Kurt was born February 27, 1967, in Aberdeen, Washington. This town is about 110 miles (177 kilometers) southwest of Seattle. Kurt's father, Don, worked as an auto mechanic. His mother, Wendy, stayed at home with Kurt and his younger sister, Kim.

Early Life

Music was a part of Kurt's life from an early age. Some of his aunts and uncles played music professionally. At age 4, Kurt amazed one of his aunts. He sat down at the piano and made up words to a song.

Learn about:

Kurt's childhood

Difficult teenage years

Turning to music

Kurt enjoyed playing music throughout his life.

Kurt's work received praise, but it made him uncomfortable.

Kurt also liked to draw. But his talent came with a problem that haunted Kurt all his life. Kurt was never satisfied with his creations.

When Kurt was in second grade, one of his drawings was chosen for the cover of the school newspaper. Instead of being happy, Kurt was upset. He didn't think his drawing was good. Praise almost always made him uncomfortable.

Kurt's high energy was another problem. He had trouble concentrating and sitting still in school. His parents took him to a doctor, who said Kurt had attention deficit disorder. The doctor gave Kurt a drug called Ritalin to calm him down. Instead, it caused Kurt to stay awake all night. The doctor then gave Kurt other drugs called sedatives to help him sleep.

"He was basically cheerful, but there was a rage to him."
—Iris Cobain, Kurt's grandmother

Kurt had problems with drugs and alcohol during much of his life.

Some people wonder whether Kurt's drug problems began during these early years. They believe that such powerful drugs can lead to other drug use later in life. Kurt began smoking marijuana in junior high. Later, he turned to LSD, heroin, and other strong drugs.

A Shattered World

Kurt's life became even worse when he was 9. His parents divorced. It was a huge shock to Kurt. He felt abandoned, angry, and depressed.

After the divorce, Kurt didn't know where he wanted to live. He took turns living with his mother, his father, and his aunts and uncles. For a time, he stayed with his uncle Chuck Fradenburg. On Kurt's 14th birthday, Chuck gave him an electric guitar. Kurt used the guitar to express his feelings of anger and loss.

CHAPTER 3

A Star on the Rise

During high school, Kurt spent much time alone playing his guitar. He had few friends. Kurt argued often with his parents and teachers. At other times, he was quiet and withdrawn.

Kurt's mood swings led some people to suspect he had bipolar disorder. This disorder causes people to switch between periods of deep depression and high energy. Depression was common in Kurt's family. At least two of his relatives had killed themselves. Bipolar disorder can be treated, but it first must be recognized. Kurt was never treated for it.

Learn about:

Kurt's problems

Forming Nirvana

Early success

Bipolar disorder may have caused Kurt's mood swings.

Difficult Years

Bipolar disorder might explain why Kurt had so much trouble finding a permanent home. At times, neither parent wanted him to live with them. His friends and relatives also got tired of his behavior. Some nights Kurt slept in cars or cardboard boxes.

Kurt was smart, but school bored him. In 12th grade, he dropped out. Kurt began thinking about a career in music. His aunts and uncles made money playing music. Maybe he could do the same.

Dealing with Pain

Soon after quitting school, Kurt tried heroin for the first time. Kurt knew the dangers of heroin, but he said he needed relief from pain. Kurt's curved spine caused his back to ache. Bronchitis gave him coughing attacks. Worst of all, he often had sharp stomach pains.

Kurt did not trust doctors to find the causes of his illnesses. Instead, he numbed the pain with powerful drugs. His decision meant that his health would only get worse.

Kurt turned to music as a way to forget about his problems.

Focused on Music

In 1987, Kurt worked on building a career in music. By then, he had moved to Olympia, Washington. This city is near Seattle. Kurt and bass player Krist Novoselic formed a band in Olympia. They changed the band's name several times. Finally, they settled on Nirvana.

For a time, Kurt's anger was replaced by a wish to be successful. Kurt wrote all the songs for Nirvana. In 1988, the band released its first single, "Love Buzz." Nirvana's first album, *Bleach*, came out in June 1989.

Nirvana's early success gave Kurt confidence. He finally had found something he could do well. Kurt believed he would be famous one day.

"Kurt knew that the gaps between the notes are as important as the music."
—*Warren Mason, Kurt's guitar teacher*

Kurt formed Nirvana with (left to right) Jason Everman, Chad Channing, and (back) Krist Novoselic.

CHAPTER 4

Nirvana Was Not Enough

Nirvana's music fit perfectly with what was happening in Seattle. The city was about to become famous for a new kind of music called grunge. The music was loud, and the songs were about the feelings and events important to young people. A grunge fashion style also became popular. Fans dressed in flannel shirts and torn jeans.

Kurt poured his feelings into his songs. His powerful performances were hard to forget. Word about Nirvana began to spread.

Learn about:

The grunge movement

Stardom

Kurt's legacy

Nirvana was one of the first and most important grunge bands.

Tours and Troubles

In 1989, Nirvana began a tour of the United States and Europe. Kurt never liked touring. Being around other people made him uncomfortable.

Nirvana's popularity became a problem for Kurt. The more people liked his music, the more miserable he became. At times, Kurt showed his unhappiness by being rude to fans. At other times, he was polite and thoughtful. His odd behavior did not hurt the band's popularity.

The Smell of Success

In May 1991, Nirvana signed a new recording contract with Geffen Records. By December, their second album, *Nevermind*, was selling 400,000 copies a week. The song "Smells Like Teen Spirit" was a best-selling single. Nirvana was about to make Kurt a millionaire.

By 1990, Nirvana's members were Dave Grohl, Kurt, and Krist Novoselic.

Fame and money did not solve Kurt's problems. His stomach problems were getting worse. Sometimes, he coughed up blood. He spent his money on heroin and other illegal drugs to drown the pain. He still refused to see a doctor.

The Last Years

In February 1992, Kurt married rock musician Courtney Love. Their daughter, Frances Bean, was born August 18. The next day, Courtney talked Kurt out of killing himself with a gun. He was worried he could never be a good father.

Kurt was addicted to heroin but refused to get help. His drug use made him angry. His outbursts drove away people who cared about him. Kurt was slowly killing himself.

Kurt and Courtney's daughter, Frances, was born in August 1992.

By 1993, Kurt was in poor health but still toured with Nirvana.

In early 1994, Nirvana began a tour of Europe. Kurt took a drug overdose in Rome, Italy. When he returned to the United States, Kurt's friends and Courtney forced him to go to a treatment center. But Kurt left the center after only two days. A few days later, he killed himself.

Kurt's depression kept him from enjoying his life and success.

A Life Cut Short

Although Kurt died in 1994, his music and influence has lived on. Two months before Kurt's death, Nirvana recorded a song called "You Know You're Right." Nine years later, the song was released. It became a hit.

A collection of Kurt's journal writings was published in 2002. That book, *Journals*, went to number one on the best-seller list.

"I wish someone could explain to me why exactly I have no desire to learn anymore. Why I used to have so much energy and the need to search for miles and weeks for anything new and different."

—Kurt Cobain, from the book Journals

Learning from Kurt's Death

Kurt was a gifted artist, but his deep depression kept him from enjoying life. People loved him because his music was emotionally honest. That was never enough for Kurt. He never learned to love himself.

One good thing came out of Kurt's death. It attracted worldwide attention to how serious depression and other emotional disorders can be. If Kurt had received the help he needed, he might still be making great music today.

"We remember Kurt for what he was: caring, generous, and sweet."
—Krist Novoselic, Nirvana's bass player

Vendetta Red

Nirvana broke up after Kurt's death. But many of today's bands still are influenced by Nirvana's songs.

The five members of Vendetta Red are all from Washington. As teenagers, they listened to Nirvana and other Seattle grunge bands. Vendetta Red formed in 1998 and began recording in 1999. In 2003, the band released its third full-length CD, *Between the Never and the Now*. The CD included the hit song "Shatterday."

Glossary

attention deficit disorder (uh-TEN-shuhn DEH-fuh-sit diss-OR-dur)—a condition that causes people to have problems concentrating and sitting still

bipolar disorder (bye-POH-lur diss-OR-dur)—an emotional disorder that causes major mood swings

bronchitis (brong-KYE-tiss)—an illness of the throat and lungs

contradiction (kon-truh-DIK-shuhn)—something that is the opposite of what it seems to be

depression (di-PRESH-uhn)—an emotional disorder that causes people to feel sad and tired

grunge (GRUHNJ)—a style of rock music that combines punk rock and heavy metal

heroin (HAIR-oh-uhn)—an illegal, addictive drug

overdose (OH-vur-dohss)—an amount of a drug that makes a person seriously ill or kills the person

sedative (SED-uh-tiv)—a drug that makes a person quiet and calm

Read More

Crisafulli, Chuck. *Teen Spirit: The Stories Behind Every Nirvana Song.* The Stories Behind Every Song. New York: Thunder's Mouth Press, 2004.

Gracie, Andrew. *Kurt Cobain.* They Died Too Young. Philadelphia: Chelsea House, 1997.

Molanphy, Chris. *Kurt Cobain: Voice of a Generation.* New York: Barnes & Noble Books, 2003.

Internet Sites

FactHound offers a safe, fun way to find Internet sites related to this book. All of the sites on FactHound have been researched by our staff.

Here's how:
1. Visit *www.facthound.com*
2. Type in this special code **0736827005** for age-appropriate sites. Or enter a search word related to this book for a more general search.
3. Click on the **Fetch It** button.

FactHound will fetch the best sites for you!

Index